SQUIBOB

An Early California Humorist

SQUIBOB

An Early California Humorist

Foreword by Richard Derby Reynolds

Yours respectively
John P. Squibob

SQUIBOB PRESS, INC.

SAN FRANCISCO, CALIFORNIA

Published by:

Squibob ® SQUIBOB PRESS, Inc.
P. O. BOX 421523
SAN FRANCISCO, CA 94142-1523

Grateful acknowledgment is made to the Bancroft Library,
University of California, Berkeley; Mills College Library; the
San Diego Historical Society; and the Special Collections
Division, United States Military Academy Library, West Point
for permission to reprint letters, maps and photographs from
their historical archives. Reprinted by permission.

Edited by Richard Derby Reynolds
Cover design by George Mattingly
Pre-Press Photography by David Close and TINTYPES

Printed and Bound in the United States of America

ISBN 0-9618577-5-7 (case)
ISBN 0-9618577-6-5 (pbk.)

Library of Congress Catalog Card Number 89-61831

To

My Grandmother Ethel,
who told me about the Derbys of Salem,
and to my mother,
Ruth Derby,
who made the stories come alive.

ACKNOWLEDGMENT

Special thanks to the staff of the Bancroft Library, University of California, Berkeley, whose manuscript and graphic files formed the primary resource for this book. I am also grateful to Bill Sturm of the Oakland Public Library, who kindly loaned me graphics of the Gold Rush Era, as well as Greer Hardwicke of the Dedham Historical Society, who traced my family tree and who chanced across a rare and previously unpublished photograph of George Horatio Derby.

During the course of this project the California Historical Society underwent severe financial problems and closed its library doors. Fortunately, much of the Derby material reposes in other collections, but the temporary loss of California Historical Society's collection could have been a disaster had the curators at the Bancroft and other librarians not filled the gap. Therefore, I would also like to thank Captain Robert Hill of the U.S. Military Academy at West Point; Patricia Akres of the San Francisco City Archives; Martin Antonetti, Special Collections Librarian, Mills College, Oakland, California; Larry Booth of the San Diego Historical Society; and Mary Allely of the San Diego Public Library who opened the vault and allowed me the luxury of reading the letters from Derby's widow to John Cheney, editor of the Caxton Club's edition of *Phoenixiana (1897)*. The San Diego Library possesses a nearly complete edition of the San Diego *Herald*, and reading these papers, in their fragile, original form was an experience I shall not forget.

Finally, I wish to posthumously thank Francis P. Farquhar of Grabhorn Press and Professor George R. Stewart who spent years meticulously researching the life and times of George Horatio Derby. After simultaneously publishing their books on Derby in 1937, Stewart and Farquhar kindly deposited their original notes, collected Derby letters, and drawings to the Bancroft Library, University of California, Berkeley. Their research provided me with a much needed lightpost when I began this project.

7

CONTENTS

"In the Name of the Prophet — FIGS."

Lt. George Horatio Derby, 1846

Derby Wharf, Courtesy The Essex Institute, Salem, Mass.

—❖ FOREWORD ❖—

When I was young, I remember my grandmother's stories about the great Derby family of Salem, Massachusetts. The windows in my childhood home were draped in a pattern showing the Derby ships that sailed from Salem across the seas to Sumatra, Canton, and the East Indies. A Civil War sword belonging to my great grandfather Captain Putnam Tarrant Derby hung heavily on the wall of my room, and my mother was forever reminding me that I had Derby blood in my Yankee veins and had been named after Captain Richard Derby, the daring sea captain, whose son, Elias Hasket, was America's "first millionaire."

Another one of my distant relatives was George Horatio Derby, a lieutenant in the U.S. Army Topographical Corps, who explored the West during the 1850's and became one of America's first humorists. My blood relationship to Lt. George Horatio Derby — even though remote — was certainly an honor. For the most part, the Derbys were colony founders, pragmatic merchants, and fiercely independent, no-nonsense sea captains who explored the trade routes from Russia to the China Sea. George Derby epitomized the best of their talents. A graduate of West Point, Lt. Derby came to California during the Gold Rush and explored the incredible wilderness of California during the early 1850's. He dammed the San Diego River and built roads through the Indian territories of Oregon and Washington. Beyond his military accomplishments, however, Derby was also a prankster, and it was this dual existence as an army officer and "wag" which enabled him to see life on two planes and write in a burlesque style that no one had ever seen before.

But George Derby died at an early age of thirty-eight, and it was rumored that he spent the last years of his life in a lunatic asylum, staring blankly at a wall, hearing and seeing no one. When George Horatio Derby passed away on May 15, 1861, newspapers reported that Derby died of insanity and had fallen victim to a mean streak of madness that he inherited from his father. It wasn't true. He probably suffered from an undiagnosed brain tumor, but because of Derby's reputation for pulling pranks of unbridled absurdity, the rumors persisted, and they illustrate how legends grew up around this great prankster of California.

If one were to dig deeply into the genealogical chasm, one would find that — like most grand families — there are "quirks" in the family blood, and the family tree is spotted with tooth carvers and non-conformists who were repeatedly fined by their Puritan brethren for refusing to observe the Sabbath. Even Captain Richard Derby and his son Elias Hasket were outspoken rebels during the American Revolution.

Likewise, George Horatio was a "wag from the womb," and contemporaries say he seemed to have inherited some wild, rebellious strain of Derby blood from his father, John Barton Derby, who was born in 1792 during the heyday of the Derby era when the wharves of Salem reeked of spice. During this lucrative period the entire town seemed to revolve around the Derby Wharf where Elias Hasket Derby Sr., affectionately known as "King Derby" because of his regal wealth, strolled in his diamond-buckled coat.

But instead of following the mercantile tradition, George's father — the grandson of "the richest man in America" — became an eccentric who wrote poetry. In 1820 John Derby left Salem for Dedham, some thirty miles west, where he married Mary Townsend, daughter of the clerk of the Courts of Norfolk County. George Horatio Derby was born from this union on April 3, 1823, but a year later John Derby deserted the family and moved to Boston to practice law and dabble in politics. The elder Derby's political views bordered on zealotry. He despised John Quincy Adams and pinned his future hopes on President Andrew Jackson, who promised to appoint him surveyor of the Port of Boston. Acting upon the promise, George's father sold his law office, all the furnishings, and gave a bond to the purchaser that he would no longer practice law. When President Jackson reneged on his promise, John Barton Derby was ruined.

Unable to practice law, George's father lived the remainder of his life as a tramp, buttonholing Bostonians with tales of his Salem ancestors, borrowing money, and hawking razor blades on the streets of Boston.

Thus, in stark contrast to the family's opulence, Mary Townsend Derby and her two-year-old son George were left in poverty. Mrs. Derby moved in with her mother and two unmarried sisters in Medfield, where she portrayed herself to staid suburban Boston society as a "widow." George was thus brought up in a maternal environment committed to eliminating any eccentricities he might have inherited from his father. But suppressing the native rebelliousness in George's personality and finding some "useful occupation" for George Horatio Derby was difficult. As a child he was unruly, prone to play pranks, and liked to draw caricatures of his friends at the School for Moral Discipline, which he attended. Even the puritanical discipline of Boston society couldn't iron out the quirks. An individual who knew young George as an apprentice in a cabinet factory remarked that he was the most "reckless and rollicking apprentice ever heard within its walls. No one could help liking him, and yet his employers were at their wits end to keep him from demoralizing the whole corps of workmen. There was no end to his pranks and eccentricities as a boy, and you could hear his laugh ringing at all hours, and most often when restraint was most appropriate."

By tapping into the Derby family's connections, Mary Townsend was able to secure George's appointment to West Point, and he entered the academy in 1842. A military career was an odd vocation for a merry prankster, but Derby seemed to have developed a split personality. In his letters to his mother from West Point, George sometimes referred to himself as "Derby and I" and it seemed as if one facet of Derby's personality craved discipline — which the U.S. Army could provide — while another personality developed into the merry prankster and "mad wag."

It was a propitious time for those cadets entering the academy. Officers in George's class of 1846 — such as George McClellan of Pennsylvania, Stonewall Jackson, and Pickett of Virginia — would later serve in the Mexican War, conquer the West, and lead the armies in this country's Civil War. Despite this stiff competition, Derby's bright mind and quick wit earned marks that placed him near the top of his class. By the end of his first year he had earned his corporal stripes, although he would later lose those stripes for his practical jokes and cartoons of the professors.

Derby's antics at West Point cost him his chevrons and became military legend, to be repeated for decades by West Pointers such as General U.S. Grant. For his lampooning and firecracker wit, Derby earned his nickname "Squibob," perhaps taken from the word "*squib*," the explosive device on a shell, which had a secondary connotation of a humorous or satirical speech. The nickname seemed to fit, for like his mother, Cadet Derby was quick to spot pretentiousness. But Derby's quick tongue also caused problems, and on one occasion his remarks so infuriated another cadet that it resulted in a duel. Derby was seriously wounded and rushed to the hospital where he lay for three weeks unable to eat or speak. But as Derby lay in the hospital he became acquainted with the surgeon who had closed his wounds. Dr. Charles McPhail Hitchcock became Derby's "earliest, closest, and most constant friend" and their destinies would cross again.

At graduation Cadet Derby received his commission in Ordnance, but within six weeks he was transferred to the elite "Topographical Engineers," a corps of officers whose map-

Derby as a young Cadet at West Point, circa 1844-1845
Photograph Courtesy The San Diego Historical Society

making and engineering talents would chart the vast frontier of the growing country. His first assignment was to survey the New Bedford Harbor and he returned to Boston in his new uniform with epaulettes of gold oak leaves and bright blue trousers. Derby's assignment in Massachusetts was followed by drafting work at the military headquarters in Washington. On December 11, 1846, orders came for Derby to proceed to Brazos, in the Gulf of Mexico, and report to General Scott for service in the war against Mexico.

After traveling by stage and steamer, Derby arrived at the desolate, lizard-infested island of Brazos, the temporary headquarters of the army of invasion. After Vera Cruz capitulated to the Americans, General Scott pushed on to Cerro Gordo, where the general halted his attack for two days as two West Pointers — Captain Robert E. Lee and Brevet Lt. George Derby — reconnoitered the enemy's position. While Lee formulated a plan for turning the Mexican's left flank, Lt. Derby crawled through the chaparral and cactus until he was able to view the Mexican lines in reverse. Derby calculated the guns and number of the enemy, and then used his drafting skills to draw a sketch of the battlefield. The attack of April 17 is dramatically described by Derby:

> "The brigade under brave Col. Harney was immediately ordered to charge and it did charge, and being attached to it myself I charged with it. About half way up, my horse was shot and fell under me with a ball through his hind leg and I had to tie him up to a tree and foot it up the rest of the way which was far preferable as the hill was so steep it was almost impossible to ride. We drove the Mexicans from the 1st hill to the 2nd hill, racing after them hollering and yelling like wild Indians, which last scared them as much as the firing. They made a stand here, but we soon drove them down with a loss of sixty killed and 140 wounded. I shot one fellow with a pistol who was about firing. He fell and begged for his life. I told him to lay still and nobody would touch him and went on. But when I came back after the fight to help

him I found somebody had killed him. He was some sort of officer and I took his sword and have got it somewhere now...

"We occupied this hill that night and lay on our blankets. The Mexicans firing grape shot & canister over us occasionally but with very little effect. Meanwhile by great exertion the ordnance had got two 12 pdrs and a 24 to the top of the hill (which was only 300 yards from Sierra Guarda) and at sunrise we opened on them for two hours. They returned our fire with interest, blazing away from 8 heavy pieces and creating horrible havoc. Capt. Mason here lost his leg, Lieut. Davis was killed. Ewell, Patten, Jarvis, Dana and others were severely wounded and all was confusion. Then Col. Harney gave the order to charge! and rushed forward himself with Lieuts. Van Dorn, Oakes, and myself by his side. With a wild hurra, the third and seventh infantry supported by the rifles rushed over the hill.

"Down we went through the whistling balls and crashing grape, men dropping here and there, the wounded groaning, but nobody scared, and with a tremendous yell we gained the ravine and commenced the ascent of Sierra Guarda.

"A fire, close, heavy and continued, from 1,800 muskets was opened on us, but the ascent was so extremely precipitous that it afforded us protection, for most of the balls passed over our heads. The whistling was terrific, the air seemed alive with balls, but we went on cheering and returning the fire now and then, when we stopped for an instant to rest. At last we came to the highest crest within ten rods of their first breastwork. We gave one fire, then Col. Harney shouted with a voice like a trumpet, 'Forward, boys! Forward! Remember the dead and give it to 'em.' Away we went.

"The Mexicans saw us coming. Nothing could withstand such a charge, they gave one fire and ran. We followed, clambered up over the breastwork, chased them from the tower, over the hill, turned their own pieces on them, and the Sierra Guarda was ours. Up went the American flag and down came the Mexican.

"It was at this moment that a retreating party going down turned and fired. I had discharged both pistols and was standing on a little knoll directing a cannon at this same party, when I felt myself struck — I fell in the arms of a kind fellow, named Buttrick of the rifle regt. who has been with me night and day ever since. The victory *was complete, seeing us in the rear the whole army surrendered and Santa Anna ran away. We took 5 Generals, 30 Cols., 5,000 men, 30 pieces of artillery and thus ended the greatest fight of the age, probably.*

"I had my wounds dressed and at 5 o'clock was brought down to this place in a litter."

Derby was lucky; his wound did not infect, which was usually the case in field wounds of the era. The musket ball that struck Derby's left hip turned on the bone and went around the thigh, and the attending surgeon decided that it would be too dangerous to remove it. Derby was sent home to recuperate in Medfield, where his proud mother met him at the railway station.

The Mexican War ended in 1847, and upon signing the Treaty of Guadalupe Hidalgo the United States fulfilled its "Manifest Destiny" and gained possession of land stretching from California to the Rio Grande. The time-table for settlement was accelerated with the discovery of gold in California, and after a stint exploring the Upper Mississippi River, Derby was immediately ordered to proceed to San Francisco to survey, chart and build roads across the newly acquired gold regions of California.

Lieutenant Derby arrived at Monterey, California on June 10, 1849, and over the next two years Derby explored the length of California from the Feather River to the tule swamps of the lower San Joaquin Valley. Derby's reports, which were published by Congress, make fascinating reading. Although primarily written in a straight-forward narrative, the lieutenant's lucid descriptions of the fertile valleys of California are sprinkled with remarks which would later characterize the writings of "Squibob." Derby joked about the dreary progress his mules made across the uncharted reaches of the Sacramento Valley, and as Derby and his companions examined the placer mines of the Mother Lode, he cynically noted that the proprietors of the barrooms were accumulating more gold than the actual collectors. Along the rivers which they were forced to cross, Derby also observed the "wretched Indians, playfully termed Christian" as they feasted on pulverized grasshoppers. In his report to General Riley he described a squaw wearing a fluffy petticoat which made her look like a "magnified pincushion." Derby also judged the dry San Joaquin Valley "entirely unfitted for agriculture" and predicted that the myriads of mosquitos along the San Joaquin River would prevent anyone from settling in the region. Even Derby, with his vivid imagination, could not imagine the grand system of canals that would drain the swamps and turn the region into California's breadbasket.

In April and May, 1850 the region around Bakersfield was a swamp-infested quagmire, but Derby fought his way through the tule reeds and mapped the Tulare Valley for later settlers. He also explored the coastal mountain ranges in the vicinity of San Luis Obispo, and then returned to bustling San Francisco, which was filled with gold-fever crazed immigrants. In 1850, half the population of San Francisco seemed to live in tents along the muddy trails that were named after the young country's heroes. But the city boasted dozens of saloons, bawdy houses, and even literary saloons like Barry & Patten's, "the favorite resort of wits, literati, and savants." Here the educated young lieutenant from West Point probably met John Nugent of the San Francisco *Herald* and Judson Ames, the future publisher of the San Diego *Herald*. It was only natural that Derby would start writing for the local newspapers during the fall of 1850. His brilliant conversation was known to stop passersby in their tracks and soon attracted the attention of other early California humorists like Stephen Massett and Alonzo Delano. According to contemporaries, Derby's memory was so phenomenal that he could recall entire conversations and passages of the Bible.

Derby was a caricaturist and *farceur,* and he began writing in a mixture of the real and imagined, in a style of humor that was unheard of in California or in American literature. It was a different kind of humor, a diametrical shift from the stuffy reportage of the mid-Nineteenth Century. Derby wrote in an exaggerated sense of the burlesque that was filled with incongruities of speech and western colloquialisms. Some of his writings, such as "The Legend of the Tehama House," is a taste of the humor Samuel Clemens would fine-tune into what critics call "western humor." Indeed, Mark Twain, who was not destined to arrive in California for another decade, later called Derby "The first of the great modern humorists." The great master of western humor acknowledged Derby's contribution by stealing a few of his best jokes.

Derby, who wrote under the pen name of "Squibob," and later "John Phoenix," was a vivacious prankster immensely popular with the pioneers in the decade following the Gold Rush. His writings, published in *Phoenixiana (1856)* went through some twenty-six printings, and had he not died at an early age one wonders what would have developed from his great literary talents. Yet, despite his popularity with the pioneers, the writings of Squibob have slipped into oblivion, and today copies of his books, *Phoenixiana* (1856) and the *Squibob Papers* (1865) are extremely rare. There have been reprints, but the last major effort to edit Derby's writings was in 1937, when Francis Farquhar of Grabhorn Press published a limited edition for collectors of Early Californiana.

When I learned that the delicious and titillating humor of *Phoenixiana* and the *Squibob Papers* was no longer readily available, I decided to republish them. In the present volume I have collected what I feel are the best of his writings from *Phoenixiana* and the *Squibob Papers*, and I have returned to the original newspapers and magazines of the day such as *The Pioneer* and *Knickerbocker* to add new material. Wherever possible, I have briefly annotated the events surrounding their publication with biographical details. To facilitate reading, I have also taken the liberty of removing a few of the hyphens prevalent in the old newspapers, changed some capitalization, and broken up long paragraphs when it seemed appropriate. Scholars of early California history should, of course, go to the source — the original newspapers such as the *Alta California* or the *Herald*.

Although some of his early California references are no longer understood, one can still savor Derby's humor in even the most badly edited newspaper articles. Derby lambasted phrenology, dentists, political appointments, tax collectors, the code of duelling, the land speculators, and other sacred institutions of the West. Squibob even had the audacity to ridicule the Secretary of War's proposed military uniforms — which almost got him court-martialed.

"Squibob in Benicia" was the first of a series of Derby "Squibs" ridiculing the flea-bitten towns of the new frontier and their pompous politicians. In this first selection, "the Veritable Squibob" pokes fun at the new California State Capitol in Benicia which dared to challenge the upstart, windswept village of San Francisco.

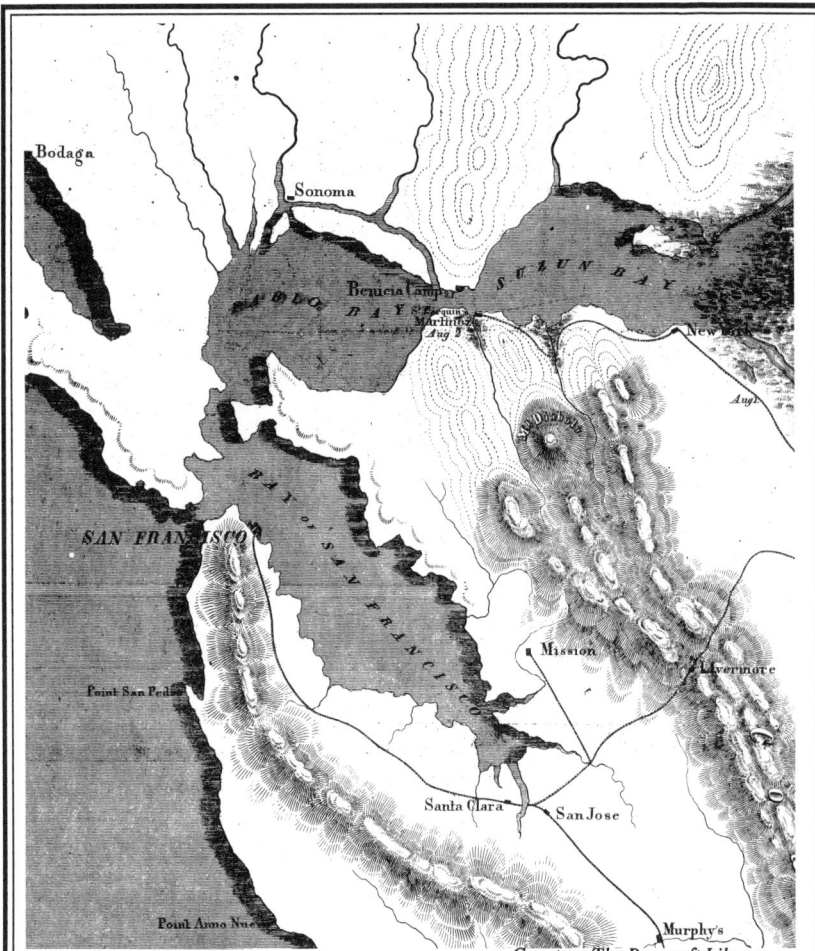

Benicia was founded in 1847 by General Mariano Vallejo, who named this settlement on the Sacramento River in honor of his wife Francisca Benicia. Benicia served as a State Capitol from 1853 to 1854, but was quickly eclipsed by the City of San Francisco. Early residents complained that although Benicia had a good harbor, it was a windy, treeless mistake, and even in 1850, Benicia's self-importance was a joke, as this letter by Derby to the *Alta California* implies.

SQUIBOB IN BENICIA

First printed in the Alta California, October 3, 1850

BENICIA, **October 1st, 1850.** Leaving the metropolis last evening by the gradually-increasing-in-popularity steamer, *West Point,* I skeeted up Pablo Bay with the intention of spending a few days at the world-renowned seaport of Benicia. Our Captain (a very pleasant and gentlemanly little fellow, by the way,) was named Swift, our passengers were emphatically a fast set, the wind blew like well-watered rose bushes, and the tide was strong in our favor. All these circumstances tended to impress me with the idea that we were to make a wonderfully quick passage, but alas, "the race is not always to the Swift," the *Senator* passed us ten miles from the wharf, and it was nine o'clock and very dark at that, when we were roped in by the side of the "ancient and fish-like" smelling hulk that forms the broad wharf of Benicia.

As I shouldered my carpet bag, and stepped upon the wharf among the dense crowd of four individuals that were there assembled, and gazing upon the mighty city whose glimmering lights, feebly discernible through the Benician darkness, extended over an area of five acres, an over-powering sense of the grandeur and majesty of the great rival of San Francisco affected me. I felt my own extreme insignificance, and was fain to lean upon a pile of watermelons for support. "Boy!" said I, addressing an intelligent specimen of humanity who formed an integral portion of the above-mentioned crowd, "Boy! Can you direct me to the best hotel in this city?"

"Ain't but one," replied the youth, "Winn keeps it; right up the hill thar."

Decidedly, thought I, I will go in to Winn, and reshouldering my carpet bag, I blundered down the ladder, upon a plank foot-path leading over an extensive morass in the direction indicated, but noticing in my abstraction that I had inadvertently retained within my grasp the melon upon which my hand rested.

"*Saw yer!*" resounded from the wharf as I retired — "*Saw yer!*" repeated several individuals upon the foot-path. For an instant my heart beat with violence at the idea of being seen accidentally appropriating so contemptible an affair as a watermelon; but hearing a man with a small white hat, and large white moustache, shout "hello!" and immediately rush with frantic violence up the ladder, I comprehended that Sawyer was his proper name, and by no means alluded to me or my proceedings; so slipping the melon in my carpet bag, I tranquilly resumed my journey.

A short walk brought me to the portal of the best and only hotel in the city, a large two-story building dignified by the title of the "Solano Hotel," where I was graciously received by mine host, who welcomed me to Benicia in the most *winning* manner. After slightly refreshing my inner man with a feeble stimulant, and undergoing an introduction to the oldest inhabitant, I calmly seated myself in the bar-room, and contemplated with intense interest the progress of a game of billiards between two enterprising citizens; but finding after a lapse of two hours, that there was no earthly probability of its ever being concluded, I seized a candlestick and retired to my room. Here I discussed my melon with intense relish, and then seeking my couch, essayed to sleep. But, oh! The fleas! Skipping, hopping, crawling, biting!

"Won't someone establish an agency for the sale of D.L. Charles Co.'s Flea Bane in Benicia?" I agonizingly shouted, and an echo answered through the reverberating halls of the Solano Hotel, "Yes, they won't."

What a night! But everything must have an end (circles and California gold excepted), and day at last broke over Benicia. Magnificent place! I gazed upon it from the attic window of the Solano Hotel, with feelings too deep for utterance. The sun was rising in its majesty, gilding the red wood shingles of the U.S. Storehouses in the distance; seven deserted hulks were riding majestically at anchor in the bay; clothes-lines with their burdens were flapping in the morning breeze; a man with a wheelbarrow was coming down the street! Everything, in short, spoke of the life, activity, business and bustle of a great city. But in the midst of the excitement of this scene, an odoriferous smell of beef-steak came like a holy calm across my olfactories, and hastily drawing in my *cabeza*, I descended to breakfast.

This operation concluded, I took a stroll in company with the oldest inhabitant, from whom I obtained much valuable information (which I hasten to present), and who cheerfully volunteered to accompany me as a guide, to the lions of the city. There are no less than forty-two wooden houses — many of them two-stories in height — in this great place, and nearly twelve hundred inhabitants — men, women and children! There are six grocery, provision, drygoods, auction, commission, and where-you-can-get-almost-any-little-thing-you-want stores, one hostel, one schoolhouse — which is also a *brevet* church — three billiard tables, a post-office — from which I actually saw a man get a letter — and a ten-pin-alley, where I am told a man once rolled a whole game, paid $1.50 for it, and walked off chuckling. Then there is a "monte bank,"

27

a Common Council, and a mayor, who my guide informed me was called "Carne," from a singular habit he has of eating roast beef for dinner. But there isn't a tree in all Benicia.

"There was one," said the guide, "last year — only four miles from here, but they chopped it down for firewood for the 'post.' Alas! Why didn't they spare that tree?

The dwelling of one individual pleased me indescribably — he had painted it a vivid green! Imaginative being. He had evidently tried to fancy it a tree, and in the enjoyment of this sweet illusion had reclined beneath its grateful shade, secured from the rays of the burning sun, and in the full enjoyment of rural felicity even among the crowded streets of this great metropolis.

How pretty is the map of Benicia! We went to see that, too. It's all laid off in squares and streets, for ever so far, and you can see pegs stuck in the ground at every corner, only they are not exactly in a line, sometimes. And there is Aspinwall's wharf where they are building a steamer of iron, that looks like a large pan, and there is Semple Slip, all divided on the map by lines and dots, into lots of incredible value; but just now they are all under water, so no one can tell what they are actually worth.* Oh! Decidedly Benicia is a great place.

"And how much, my dear sir," I modestly inquired of the gentlemanly recorder who displayed the map; "How much may this lot be worth?" And I pointed with my finger at lot No. 97, block 16,496, situated as per map in the very center of the swamp.

"That sir," replied he with much suavity, "Ah! It would be held at about three thousand dollars, I suppose." I shuddered — and retired.

---

* Editor's Note — Derby knew all about speculative lots. In October, 1849 he surveyed and mapped out the gold-mining town of Kearny, on the Bear River, complete with a public square and 262 lots with "excellent soil for gardening." For his effort, Derby was paid with vacant lots, which turned out to be worthless when no gold was found in the vicinity.

Squibob in Benicia

The history of Benicia is singular. The origin of its name as related by the oldest inhabitant is remarkable. I put it right down in my notebook as he spoke, and believe it religiously, every word.

"Many years ago," said that aged man, "this property was owned by two gentlemen, one of whom from his extreme candor and ingenuousness of character we will call Simple; the other being distinguished for waggery and a disposition for practical joking, I shall call — as in fact he was familiarly termed in those days — Larkin. While walking over the grounds in company, on one occassion, and being naturally struck by its natural advantages, said Simple to Larkin: "Why not make a city here, my boy? Have it surveyed into squares, bring up ships, build houses, make it a port of entry, establish depots, sell lots, and knock the center out of Yerba Buena straight.' (Yerba Buena is now San Francisco, reader.) 'Ah! quoth Larkin with a pleasant grin diffusing itself over his agreeable countenance, "that would be nice, hey?'" Need we say that the plan was adopted, carried out, proved successful, and Larkin's memorable remark, "*be nice, hey*," adopted as the name of the growing city, gradually became altered and vulgarized into its present form — Benicia! A curious history this, which would have delighted Horne Took beyond measure.

Having visited the Masonic Hall,* which is really a large and beautiful building, reflecting credit alike on the architect and fraternity, being by far the best and most convenient hall in the country, I returned to the Solano Hotel where I was accosted by a gentleman in a blue suit with many buttons, and a sanguinary streak down the leg of his trousers, whom I almost immediately recognized as my old friend, Captain George P.

---

* Editor's Note — Derby was a conscientious Mason. Information about Derby's Masonic activities can be found in John Whicher's *Masonic Beginnings in California and Hawaii* (1931), and in Cyrus Field Willard's *The Master Mason*.

Squibob

Lambs, of the U.S. Artillery, a thorough-going *adobe*, as the Spaniard has it, and a member in high and regular standing of the Dumfudgin Club. He lives in a delightful little cottage, about a quarter of a mile from the center of the city — being on duty at the Post — which is some mile, mile and a half or two miles from that metropolis — and pressed me so earnestly to partake of his hospitality during my short sojourn, that I was at last fain to pack up my property, including the remains of the abstracted melon, and in spite of the blandishments of my kind host of the Solano, accompanied him to his domicile, which he very appropriately names "Mischief Hall." So here I am installed for a few days, at the expiration of which I shall make a rambling excursion to Sonoma, Napa and the like, and from whence perhaps you may hear from me. As I sit here looking from my airy chamber, upon the crowds of two or three persons, thronging the streets of the great city; as I gaze upon that man carrying home a pound and a half of fresh beef for his dinner; as I listen to the bell of the *Mary* (a Napa steam packet of four cat power) ringing for departure, while her captain in a hoarse voice of authority requests the passengers to "step over the other side, as the larboard paddlebox is underwater;" as I view all these unmistakable signs of the growth and prosperity of Benicia, I cannot but wonder at the infatuation of the people of your village, who persist in their absurd belief that San Francisco will become a *place*, and do not hesitate to advance the imbecile idea that it may become a successful rival of this city. Nonsense! — Oh, Lord! At this instant there passed by my window the — prettiest — little — I can't write any more this week; if this takes, I'll try again.

Yours for ever,

Squibob

Dedham Historical Society, Dedham, Massachusetts

SQUIBOB IN SONOMA

First printed in the Alta California, October 21, 1850

SONOMA, **October 10, 1850.** I arrvived at this place some days since, but have been so entirely occupied during the interval in racing over the adjacent hills in pursuit of unhappy partridges, wandering along the banks of the beautiful creek, whipping its tranquil surface for speckled trout, or cramming myself with grapes at the vineyard, that I have not, until this moment, found time to fulfil my promise of a continuation of my traveling adventures.

I left Benicia with satisfaction. Ungrateful people! I had expected, after the very handsome manner in which I had spoken of their city; the glowing description of its magnitude, prosperity and resources that I had given, the consequent rise in property that had taken place; the manifest effect that my letter would produce upon the action of Congress in making Benicia a port of entry; in view of all these circumstances I had, indeed, possibly, or peradventure a delicate present of a lot or two the deeds enclosed in a neat and appropriate letter from the Town Council. But no! The name of Squibob remains unhonored and unsung, and, what is far worse, unrecorded and untaxed in magnificent Benicia. How sharper than a serpent's thanks it is to have a toothless child, as Pope beautifully remarks in his **Paradise Lost.** One individual characterized my letter as a 'd...d burlesque.'

I pity that person and forgive him.

For the last few days of my stay in Benicia, the city was in a perfect whirl of excitement. The election* was rapidly approaching, and Herr Rossiter was exhibiting feats of legerdemain at the California House. Individuals were rushing about the streets proferring election tickets of all shapes and sizes, and tickets for the exhibition were on sale at all the principal hotels. One man conjured you to take a ticket, while another asked you to take a ticket to see the man conjured, so that what, with the wire-pulling by day, and the slack wire performance by night, you stood an excellent chance for getting slightly bewildered. Public meetings were held, where multitudes of fifty excited individuals surrounded the steps of the El Dorado, listening with breathless interest to a speech in favor of McDaniels, and abusive to Bradford, or in favor of somebody else and everlastingly condemnatory of both. Election meetings, anywhere, are always exciting and interesting spectacles, but the moral effect produced by the last which I attended in Benicia, when (after some little creature named Frisbie had made a speech, declaring his readiness to wrap himself in the Bar-Stangled Spanner, fire off a pistol, and die like a son of ... Liberty, for the Union). Dr. Simple slowly unfolded himself to his utmost height, and with one hand resting upon the chimney of the El Dorado, and the other holding his *serape* up to Heaven, denounced such sentiments, and declaring that California had made him, and he should go his

* Editor's Note — John Bigler was elected the governor of California in 1850 and later became a primary target of Squibob's political barbs.

length for California, right or wrong union or disunion. The moral effect produced, I say, was something more exciting; it was sublime; it was tremendous!

"That's a right-down good speech," said my fair companion; "but my! How the General gave it to him. Didn't he, Mr. Squibob?"

"He did so," said I.

The candidates were all Democrats, I believe, and all but one entertained the same sentiments. This gentleman (a candidate for the Senate), however, in the elucidation of his political principals, declared that he "went in altogether for John C. Calhoun, and nothing shorter."

Now I'm no politican, and I have no wish to engage in a controversy on the subject; but, God forgive me if I am in error, I thought Calhoun had been dead for some months. Well, I suppose someone is elected by this time, and the waves of political excitement have become calm, but Benicia was a stormy place during the election, I assure you. I succeeded in borrowing one dollar at ten per cent a month (with security on a corner lot in Kearny Street, San Francisco), purchased a ticket and went to see Herr Rossiter. Gracious! How he balanced tobacco pipes, and tossed knives in the air, and jumped on a wire, and sat down on it, and rolled over it, and made it swing to and fro while he threw little brass balls from one hand to the other. The applause was tremendous, and when, after a solo by the orchestra (which consisted of one seedy violin, played by an individual in such a state of hopeless inebriation that his very fiddle seemed to hiccough), he threw a back-handed summerset, and falling a graceful attitude, informed the audience that "he should appear again tomorrow evening with a change of performance."

We enthusiastically cheered, and my friend, the man in the red vest who had sat during the whole evening in a state of rapt admiration, observed with a profound ejaculation, "that it went ahead of anything he had ever seen in his life, except the Falls of Niagara!"

I made many friends in Benicia. I don't like the place much, but I do like the people; and among my acquaintances from Mr. Simple to my friend Mr. Sawyer, which two gentlemen may be termed the long and short of the place, I have never met with more kindness, more genuine hospitality than from the gentlemen of Benicia. The ladies are pretty, too; but, to use an entirely original metaphor, which I presume none of your readers ever heard before or will hear again: they are "like angels' visits, few and far between." There isn't a more moral place on the face of the earth than Benicia. Ephesus, where the stupid people a few years since used to worship Diana, wasn't a circumstance to it.

Sonoma is twelve miles from Napa, and is — but I shall defer my description until next week, for I have scarcely made up my mind with regard to it, and my waning paper warns me I have said enough at present.

Yours for ever.

Squibob in San Francisco

First Printed in the Alta California, October 29, 1850

SAN FRANCISCO, **October 15th, 1850.** Time! At the word Squibob comes cheerfully up to the scratch, and gracefully smiling upon his friends and supporters, lets fly his one, two, as follows —

Sonoma *is* a nice place. As my Sabbath school instructor (peace to his memory) used to add, by the way of a clincher to his dictum— Piety is the foundation of all Religion —"Thar can't be no doubt on't."

Situated in the midst of the delightful and fertile valley which bears its name, within three miles of the beautiful creek upon whose "silvery tide," where whilom sported the *tule* boats of the unpleasant Indians, the magnificent (ly little) steamer *Georgina* now puffs and wheezes tri-weekly from San Francisco; enjoying an unvaryingly salubrious climate, neither too warm nor too cold. With little wind, few fleas, and a sky of that peculiarly blue description, that Fremont terms *the Italian,* it may well be called, as by the sentimentally struck travelling snob it frequently is, the Garden of California. I remained there ten whole days — somewhat of a marvel for so determined a gad-about as myself — and don't remember of ever passing ten days more pleasantly. It is useless for me to occupy time, and trespass upon your patience by a lengthy description of Sonoma. If any of your readers would know the exact number of houses it contains, the names of the people who dwell therein, the botanical applications of the plants growing in its vicinity, or anything else about it that would be of any mortal use to anyone, without being positively amusing, let them purchase Revere, or some other equally scientific work on California, and inform themselves. Suffice it to say that there is delightful society, beautiful women, brave men, and most luscious grapes to be found there; and the best thing one can possibly do, if a tired and *ennuyeed* resident of San Francisco, Benicia, or any other great city of all work and no play, is to take the *Georgina* some pleasant afternoon and go up there for a change. He'll find it! General Smith and his staff reside at Sonoma, and a small detachment of troops have their station and quarters there. I saw a trooper in the street one day; he wore a coat with a singularly brief tail, and a nose of a remarkably vivid tinge of redness. I thought he might have just returned from *the* expedition, his limbs were evidently weakened by toil and privation, and his course along the street slow in movement and serpentine in direction. I would have asked him to proceed to the Sink of Mary's River, and recover an odd boot that I left there last fall, but he looked scarcely fit to make the journey. I feared he might be Jenkins, and forebore. But it's a glorious thing to reflect that we have an army at our disposal in this country, and a blessed reflection, that should we lose any old clothing in the wilderness, we can get Mr. Crawford to get that branch of the service to pick it up.

Tired at last of monotony, even in beautiful Sonoma, I packed up my carpet bag and taking the two-mule stage, passed through pretty little Napa again, and found myself, one evening, once more at Benicia. It had increased somewhat since I had left it. I observed several new clothes poles had been erected, and noticed a hand cart at the corner of a street that I had never seen before. But I had little time for observation, for the *New World* came puffing up to the hulks as I arrived, and I hastily stepped on board. Here I met my ancient crony and distinguished friend Le Baron Vieux, who was on his way from Sacramento to the metropolis. The Baron is a good fellow and a funny man. You have frequently laughed over his drolleries in the *True Delta*. In his usually unimpeachably "good style," he showed me about the boat, introduced me to the captain, pointed out the "model artists" who were on board, and finally capped the climax of his polite attention by requesting me to take a drink. I didn't refuse, particularly — and we descended to the bar.

"And what, my dear fellow," asked the Baron with a pleasant and hospitable smile,"will you drink?"

I chose *Bine* and *Witters*. The baron himself was drinking *Bin* and *Gitters*. We hob-a-nobbed, tossed off our glasses without winking, and for an instant gazed at each other in gasping, unspeakable astonishment.

"Turpentine and aqua fortis!" shuddered I.

"Friend!" said the Baron in an awful voice to the barkeeper, "that drink is fifty cents, but I will with pleasure give you a dollar to tell us *what* it was we drank."

"We call it," replied that imperturbable man,"Sherry Wine, but I don't know as I ever saw anyone drink it before."

Quoth the Baron, who was by this time had partially recovered his circulation and the consequent flow of his ideas:

"I think, my friend, you'll never see it drank before or behind, hereafter."

The *New World* is an excellent and, for California, an elegant boat. Her Captain (who don't know Wakeman?) is a pleasant gentleman. Her accommodations are unequalled — but, and I say this expressly for the benefit of my brethren of the "Dumfudgin Club," never call for "wine and bitters" at her bar.

Ascending to the cabin on the upper deck, I had the satisfaction of a formal presentation to Dr. Collyer and his interesting family. Sober, high-toned, moral and well-conducted citizens may sneer if they please; rowdies may visit, and with no other than the prurient ideas arising from their own obscene imaginations, may endorse the same opinions more forcibly by loud ejaculations and vulgar remarks; but I pretend to say that no right-minded man, with anything like the commencement of a taste for the beautiful and artistic, can attend one of these "Model Artist" exhibitions without feeling astonished, gratified, and, if an enthusiast — delighted. As our gallant boat, dashing the spray from her bow, bore us safely and rapidly onward through the lovely bay of San Pablo, the moon tipping with its silvery rays each curling wave around us, and shedding a flood of yellow light upon our upper deck, " I walked with Sappho."

"Oh, beautiful thing," said I, somewhat excited by the inspiring nature of the scene, and possibly, the least thought, by the turpentine I had imbibed, " do you never feel, when in the pride of your matchless charms you stand before us, the living, breathing representation of the lovely, poetic, and ill-fated Sappho. Do you never feel an inspiration of the moment, and, entering into the character, imagine yourself in mind, as in form, her beauteous illustration?"

"Well —yes," said she, with the slightest possible indication of a yawn, "I don't know but I do, but it's *dreadful tearing on the legs!*"

Hem! A steamer's motion always made me feel unpleasantly, and the waves of San Pablo Bay ran high that evening. The Baron and I took more turpentine immediately. We landed in your metropolis shortly after, and succeeding in obtaining a man to carry my valise a couple of squares, for which service — being late — he charged me but thirty-two dollars, I repaired to, and registered my name at the St. Francis Hotel, which being deciphered with any almost imperceptible grin by my own and every other traveller's agreeable and gentlemanly friend Campbell, I received the key of No. 12, and incontinently retired to rest.

What I have seen in San Francisco I reserve for another occassion. I leave for San Diego this evening, from which place I will take an early opportunity of addressing you. I regret that I cannot remain to be a participant in the coming celebration, but my cousin Skewball, a resident of the city, who writes with a keen, if not "caustic pen," has promised to furnish you an elaborate account of the affair, which, if you print, I trust you will send me. Write me by the post office.

Au reservoir.

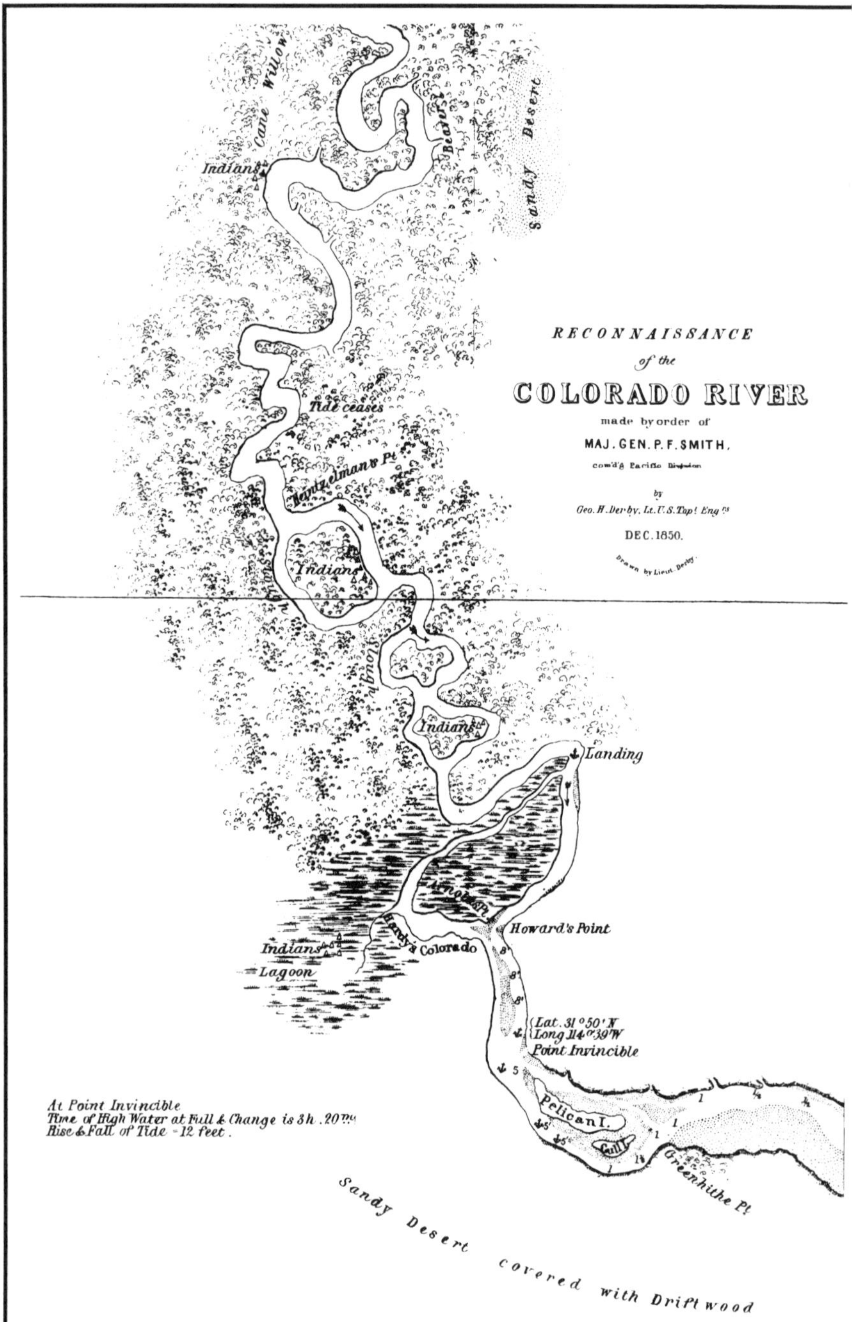

RECONNAISSANCE
of the
COLORADO RIVER
made by order of
MAJ. GEN. P. F. SMITH,
com'd'g Pacific Division

by
Geo. H. Derby, Lt. U.S. Top! Eng?s

DEC. 1850.

Drawn by Lieut. Derby

At Point Invincible
Time of High Water at Full & Change is 8 h . 20 m.
Rise & Fall of Tide ~ 12 feet .

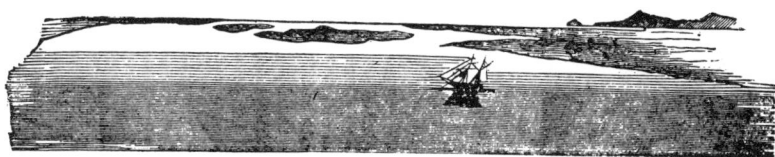

Gore I.   Montague I.   Sargent's Pt.

The Explorer

Derby's literary career was interrupted immediately after "Squibob's" debut in the *Alta California*. On October 11, 1850, Lieutenant Colonel Joseph Hooker, Adjutant General of the Pacific Division, wrote Derby that "a skilful and industrious officer is needed ... to open a route of transportation by water to the mouth of the Gila River." Like his ancestors, Brevet Lt. George Derby's destiny was the sea.

On November 1, 1850 Derby set sail from Francisco on the 120-ton topsail schooner *Invincible*, with a crew of nine seamen, a cook, a steward and two mates bound for the Gulf of California. His orders were simply to explore the lower Colorado River and establish a water supply route for the newly established army post at Fort Yuma. After stopping briefly in San Diego where the ship was loaded with supplies, the *Invincible* rounded the penisula of Lower California and anchored at the harbour of "Guyaymas."

> *We found Guyaymas a dirty place, with a dirty population of about 1,500 or 2,000. The houses being built of adobe with the roofs sloping toward the interior, have a very unfinished appearance, and from the harbour the town presents the appearance of having been abandoned when half built.*

Colonel Hooker had warned that although the Gulf of California was "infested by Indians," there could be no military escort. In fact, Lt. Derby wryly noted in his report, the ship's entire armament consisted of an old iron twelve-pounder carronade (captured from the Mexicans at Tabasco) and six flint-lock muskets. After arriving in present-day Guaymas, the Americans heard more tales of the ferocity of the Indians on the Colorado, and Derby bought two small swivel cannons and enlisted three more seamen. Then, for three weeks Derby and the crew of the *Invincible* pushed northward, battling winter-season gales. On the twenty-eighth of December they found themselves entering the narrowing waters of the Colorado in "water devoid of any brackish taste, but extremely muddy, resembling in its character that of the Mississippi River."

Derby easily assumed the role of his ancestral sea captains. He explored ahead with the whale-boat, and helped Captain Wilcox and his crew guide the schooner over the shallow shoals. The ship drew eight to nine feet of water, and at times the extreme low winter tides left the schooner stranded on the mud. At other times the strong incoming tides hemmed the ship between the Indian-haunted desert and empty, unpredictable sea. When they finally reached a split in the river where the channels were too shallow to continue, they fired their heavy guns at intervals in the hope that they might be within earshot of Major Heintzelman's command at Fort Yuma. But instead of summoning the soldiers, the guns brought fifteen Cocopas Indians to the water's edge:

> *They were very much like all other Indians, with coarse black hair, like a horse's mane, cropped straight across the eyes, and with no clothing except the inevitable dirty rag worn apron fashion about their loins; they were, however, a little nastier than any other Indians I had ever before seen, being beplastered from head to foot with mud, with which some of them had filled their hair; one had on a linen coat, and another to our great joy, an infantry great coat ... I*

ascertained from the chief they were acquainted with Major Heintzelman, and would carry a letter to him from me, which they said would take a day and a half.

Derby and his crew worked the schooner up the river another few miles and the ship anchored at a curve of land near Pelican Island which Derby named "Point Invincible." Major Heintzelman and a detail of soldiers finally appeared on the banks of the desert river and after the supplies were turned over to the soldiers from Fort Yuma, Brevet Lt. Derby and his crew returned to San Francisco.

Derby would later map the alternative wagon trails across the desert from San Diego, and his wisecracks about the oppressive heat of the region became a part of American folklore. In his mock lectures on astronomy, Derby compared Ft. Yuma to the planet Mercury:

> *"It receives six and a half times as much heat from the sun as we do; from which we conclude that the climate must be very similiar to that of Fort Yuma, on the Colorado River. The difficulty of communication with Mercury will probably prevent its ever being selected as a military post; though it possesses many advantages for that purpose, being extremely inaccessible, inconvenient, and doubtless, singularly uncomfortable."*

Another famous wisecrack, later attributed to Derby by Mark Twain:

> *"There is a tradition (attributed to John Phoenix) that a very, very wicked soldier died there once, and of course went straight to the hottest corner of perdition — and the next day he telegraphed back for his blankets."*

On March 6, 1851 Derby returned to San Francisco from his expedition to the mouth of the Colorado River, and he filed his report with Colonel Hooker. Lt. Derby had accomplished his mission, and his report would be published by the Senate. Derby's exploration had proved that it was feasible to navigate the mouth of the Colorado, which was preferable to the long trek by wagon trail across the sandy, waterless desert east of San Diego. Lt. Derby's success at establishing a water supply route to southeastern California helped to establish the post at Fort Yuma, and insured the American occupation of the Arizona territory.

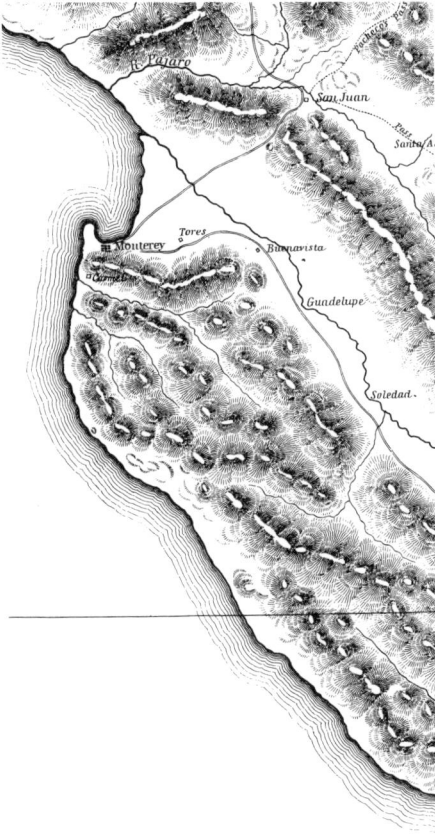

Courtesy Peter Browning

With his topographical surveys of the California gold regions, the San Joaquin Valley, and the mouth of the Colorado, Lt. George Derby could legitimately call himself "an explorer." But Derby lived a double life, and his brief writings of the previous fall and the hilarious exploits of "Squibob" had also established Derby's dual identity as a "humorist." It was Derby, the rumor went, that first discovered that the sign "Yreka Bakery" spelled the same words, frontwards or backwards. San Francisco and frontier towns alike were still buzzing over Derby's pranks and quick wit.

Derby's pranks continued after his assignment to the Third Division, which was headquartered in Sonoma. One of his better known exploits has become an American classic of the frontier and was later interwoven into the stories of

The Virginian by Owen Wister. It began when the town of Sonoma gave a ball and families from all over the region were invited. It was customary for the mothers to leave the babies in the same room where they left their cloaks and a single person could watch after them. At some point during the night, however, someone (presumably Derby) switched the babies and changed their blankets so that at the end of the festivities the unsuspecting mothers carried off the wrong sleeping babies. Derby later wrote that upon arriving at their distant ranches, the outraged babies "would not draw their nourishment from strange maternal fountains, and were vociferous in their protestations." The panicked mothers caused such an uproar in Sonoma that Derby was obligated to pay the cost of another ball.

Lieutenant Derby's pranks in Sonoma certainly didn't help his relationship with the commanding officer Lieutenant Colonel Joseph Hooker. Later known as "Fighting Joe" of the Army of the Potomac, Colonel Hooker took a personal disliking towards Derby and his ungentlemanly pranks.

In June, 1851 an incident occurred which gave Colonel Hooker an opportunity to vent these feelings towards the wisecracking young lieutenant. The incident began when an army deserter from the dragoons named Samuel Church escaped from confinement at the Benicia guardhouse and fled to Sonoma, where he stole Derby's prized gray gelding from the public stable. Horse-stealing was popularly recognized as a capital crime in the frontier. When Derby heard that the culprit was headed for San Francisco, he wrote the secretary of the Vigilance Committee and promised that "on being informed of his arrest by your body I will appear before you, and give you evidence against him which will convince you he should no longer be allowed to cumber the earth."

Three days later the highly efficient San Francisco Vigilance Committee had Samuel Church in custody, and on July 8, 1851 they turned the horse-thief over to civil authorities in Sonoma. The local authorities placed the prisoner in Derby's office guarded by two constables.

However, as word passed through the village of Sonoma that the culprit was in custody, a lynching was set in motion.

When Derby learned that the local Vigilance Committee planned to hang Church, he suddenly had a change of heart:

> *"I had been solely instrumental in the arrest of this poor wretch. I felt sure that he would be hung if he remained in my room. I did not think his crime of sufficient magnitude to forfeit his life, & I felt that if he was hung in this manner by a lawless mob I should always consider his blood upon my head. Therefore I allowed him to escape, taking such precautions as I thought would ensure me from detection."*

When Derby's role in the escape was discovered, he was promptly arrested by the Sonoma sheriff for assisting a felon. Lieutenant Derby was also charged by the military authorities with allowing an army deserter to escape. Moreover, Hooker accused Derby of conduct unbecoming an officer because he "refrained from entering into a fight with a street ruffian who cursed and challenged him for a bout with fists." This was a strange accusation coming from a commander whose forces would later butcher Chancellorsville and whose army was followed by such legions of prostitutes that ladies of the night took on the name "hookers." But in days when dueling was popular, Derby's refusal to respond to a horse-thief's challenge was akin to cowardice in the face of duty.

Derby was convinced that Colonel Hooker had brought the military charges against him because of personal animosity. In his letters, Derby saw a "Hook — er" conspiracy everywhere, and he became confused and paranoid. Despondent over the apparent ruin of his career, Derby drank heavily, and when it seemed that even his comrades had turned informants for Hooker, Derby attempted suicide. Dr. John S. Griffin, the army surgeon, was able to pull him through, but in his delirium, Derby confessed his crimes to the doctor, thereby supplying the evidence Colonel Hooker was seeking.

Derby's salvation came from his old friend Dr. Charles Hitchcock, the army surgeon who had saved his life at West Point. Dr. Hitchcock had recently been assigned to the Pacific, and on May 20, 1851, the surgeon, his wife Martha, and their sprightly daughter Lillie arrived in San Francisco. In a letter to her sister-in-law, Mrs. Hitchcock wrote that San Francisco was "a Paradise for men" but living conditions were appalling: the streets were non-existent and residents moved about the village on wooden planks. And when a devastating fire

Dr. Charles Hitchcock
Courtesy Mills College Library

consumed the city on the 22nd of June, the Hitchcocks' eight-year-old daughter Lillie almost went beserk. Deeply affected by this horrifying experience, Lillie Hitchcock later became a compulsive fire engine chaser and especially devoted to Knickerbocker Fire Engine No. 5.

But that is another story. In November, 1851 the doctor and his family had settled into the Oriental Hotel on Bush Street. When Dr. Hitchcock received the letter from Derby, the good doctor hurried to the lieutenant's bedside in Sonoma and took complete control of the case. He secured a pledge from Derby to stop his drinking, and then persuaded Dr. Griffin to testify at Derby's court-martial that the patient's confession was the result of a disordered brain at the time of illness. Without Dr. Griffin's testimony, the prosecution collapsed and Derby was released from house arrest with a mere reprimand.

THE NEW UNIFORM.
№ 3.

Newly married Officer __ My dear is there anything particularly singular in our appearance to attract the attention of these people in this unpleasant way?

Courtesy The Bancroft Library

48

"THE NEW
UNIFORM"

In a letter to his mother dated February 12, 1852, Lt Derby wrote that he was "off the hook" in the horse theft episode and he was in favor with his superiors again. He had learned his lesson and added:

"I heard the other day that Church had been arrested again at Stockton for stealing another horse and hung, and I am very glad of it!"

Derby's next prank followed closely on the heels of the Sonoma incident. In the same letter to his mother, Derby commented on the ridiculous new uniform that the Secretary of War proposed for the army. The new regulations for the uniform were declared in General Order No. 31 on June 12, 1851, and the primary change was from the old cocked hat to a cone-shaped cap, about six inches tall with a spherical pompon, which gave the appearance of a dunce's cap. The uniform and cap were totally impractical for any kind of campaign, yet the War Department was obliged to solicit opinions from the army officers, who were to bear the cost of the new uniform.

Legend has it that Derby shut himself up in a room at Fort Yuma for two or three days and sent his drawings and explanatory text to the Secretary of War in a huge tin tube ten feet in length. The legendary drawings recommended constructing the cap from sugar-loaf paper and replacing the pompon with an orange. Ornamental hair brushes, which stuck out from the shoulders like wings, could replace the epaulets. Derby also suggested inserting a hook in the seat of each officer's pants to help keep the dragoons in their saddles and to prevent them from retreating in battle.

According to Derby legend, these insulting and ridiculous suggestions so outraged the newly-appointed Secretary of War Jefferson Davis that he proposed to court-martial the lieutenant, and was only prevented from doing so after a member of his cabinet suggested that a court-martial would draw more attention to the insult. But the historian George Stewart claims that this story is pure legend. More likely, Derby circulated his drawings among friends, and indeed, a four page pamphlet signed by Squibob soon appeared on the rowdy streets of San Francisco, mocking the proposed uniform. A second series of drawings, closely resembling Derby's design, also appeared in the April 3rd and May 1, 1852 issues of *The Carpet-Bag* while Derby was on his way back East for reassignment. These drawings would haunt Jefferson Davis even after Derby's death, and were reproduced during the Civil War to mock troops loyal to Davis when he became President of the Confederacy.

Fig. 1.

Proposed alteration in the New Uniform

1 Cap   To be of light blue paper, as per pattern. Possessing all the grace and elegance of outline of that lately adopted, it is infinitely lighter and far preferable on the score of economy, as it may be procured for a mere trifle at any grocery.

The New Uniform

Proposed Uniform.

Fig 2.   Fig 3.

3. Pantaloons. To be of light blue cloth as per pattern. The seat to be adorned with a star of yellow metal, having a strong brass hook in the centre as in Fig. 2. The use of the hook in transporting the lighter articles of the soldier's baggage upon a march. is obvious by reference to Fig. 3.

Fig. 4.

4. Grappling-Iron. Each Non-commissioned officer to be furnished with a grappling-iron as per pattern, Fig 4. Its use in arresting deserters is seen by referring to Fig. 5.

Drawings Courtesy The San Diego Historical Society — Ticor Collection

Proposed Uniform.

Fig. 5.

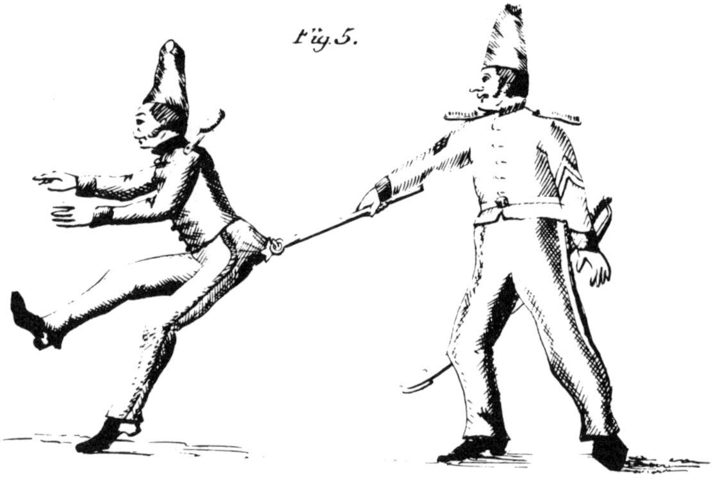

5. The advantages which the hook possesses on the score of humanity, in doing away with the objectionable punishment of "bucking" are worthy of consideration. By attaching the hook to a permanent staple in a wall, the soldier is effectually secured without doing that violence to his feelings of self respect which the passage of a stick between his legs is calculated to occasion.

6. By having a small iron rod over the hooks of the Infantry, they are kept in a perfect line, making their drill more accurate; and by attaching a small staple to the cantle of the dragoon's saddle, that valuable branch of the service might be firmly secured in their seats, and become the most fearless horsemen in the world.

No invention except Colt's Pistol has been devised so well calculated to increase the efficiency of the United States Army as this Hook.

THE DERBY DIKE

On the first of September, 1852, Lt. Derby was in Medfield "awaiting orders." When these orders finally arrived, Derby was commanded to repair to San Diego to "make a thorough and accurate survey of the locality involved in the project of building a levee across the San Diego River, for the purpose of turning it into the False Bay."

Derby's assignment would certainly bring a smile to any visitor of modern San Diego, for the river Derby was to tame is now confined to a series of cement culverts and buried beneath a commercial landscape of hotels, shopping malls and interstate freeways. But the San Diego River, which has its source in the Volcan Mountains, is deceptive. The river flows west through the El Cajon and Mission Valley before it empties into False Bay, and winter storms have sometimes turned the trickle into a raging, turbulent river, covering the entire Mission Valley floor, and sweeping everything in its path down to the sea.

Before it was finally tamed, the erratic San Diego River often shifted its path during the winter rains, and the river alternated in dumping its load of mud and silt into the False Bay and the San Diego Harbor. After severe floods during the winter of 1839-1840 filled the San Diego Harbor with large amounts of silt, settlers of the tiny San Diego village were convinced that the river's erratic nature threatened to destroy not only the safest harbor south of San Francisco

Survey of San Diego River

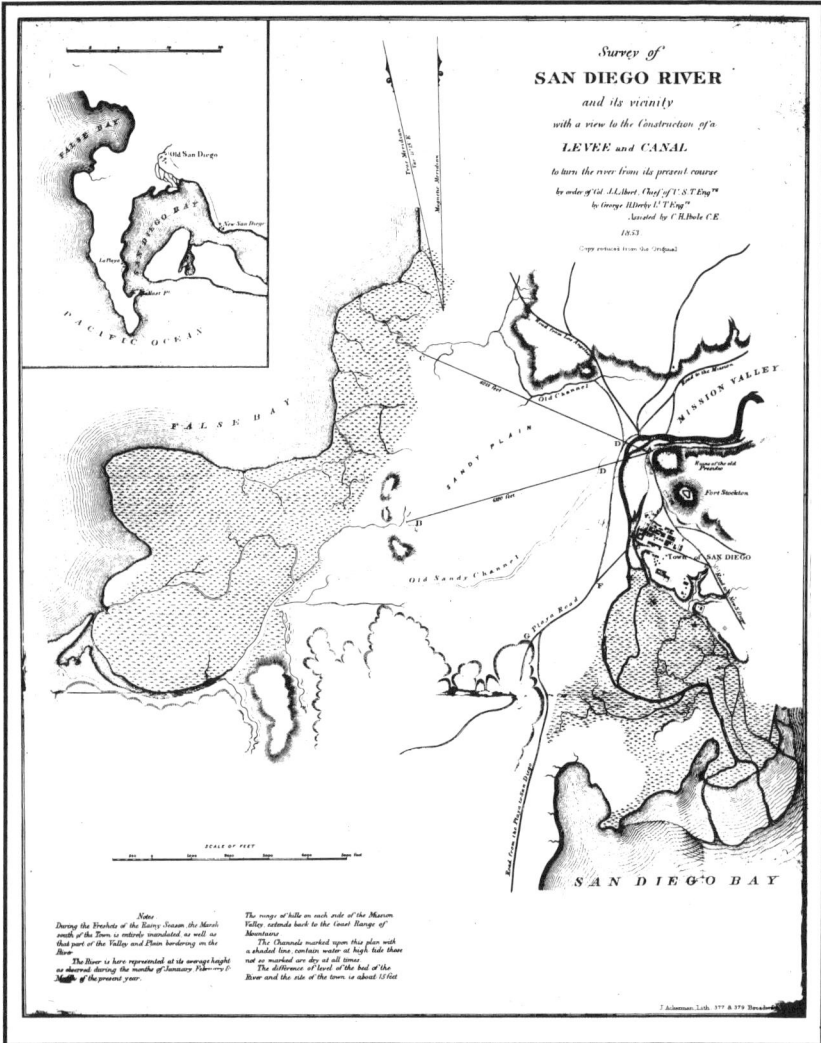

Survey of
SAN DIEGO RIVER
and its vicinity
with a view to the Construction of a
LEVEE and CANAL
to turn the river from its present course
by order of Col. J.J. Abert, Chief of U.S.T.Eng.rs
by George H.Derby Lt T.Eng.rs
Assisted by C.H.Poole C.E.
1853

Courtesy The San Diego Historical Society — Ticor Collection

54

harbor, but also their source of fresh drinking water. The residents of early San Diego bombarded Congress with petitions, and on August 30, 1852 Congress finally appropriated thirty thousand dollars for the construction of a dam to turn the river away from the harbor.

Some say that the assignment was the War Department's revenge for Derby's embarrassing cartoons of the proposed new uniforms. Jefferson Davis, the incoming Secretary of War, who had sponsored the uniforms, was particularly angry. But, in reality, Lt. Derby was probably the logical choice for the job. He was a first-rate engineer, and on earlier assignments Derby had surveyed and explored the desert east of San Diego.

Derby set sail on the 17th of November, 1852, accompanied by his friend and former classmate at West Point Charles H. Poole. Derby had persuaded Poole, who was the City Engineer of Roxbury, Massachusetts, to act as his assistant, and they arrived on New Year's Day in San Francisco, where the engineer secured instruments and passage to the town of San Diego.

By April, 1853, after three months work, Derby wrote Colonel Abert that he had completed the survey and was transmitting maps and five proposals for changing the course of the River. In Derby's mind, the only way to insure that the river permanently flowed into False Bay was to built an eight-foot high levee from the hill where the ruins of the old Presidio and Mission were located, across the river valley some 6,320 feet to where the old river channel emptied into a large slough on False Bay. But Lt. Derby knew that the appropriation by Congress was not enough to do the job correctly, so he proposed various plans, which ranged from erecting a small levee costing $20,000 to the ambitious $90,000 plan Derby knew would be required to turn the river.

After Derby shipped the plans and drawings to Colonel J. Abert in Washington, the San Diego "Dam Builder" took a vacation from the sleepy mission town and boarded a steamer for San Francisco.

On April 28th, 1853, while he waited for the War Department's decision on the San Diego River proposal, Lt. Derby left San Diego and sailed for San Francisco. He established himself at the Tehama House, a boarding house for bachelor officers, and immediately changed the menu to include such delicacies as rat-tail soup and kangaroo cutlet. In another famous incident — which seems to have been repeated with various players — Derby introduced two women, and whispered to each of them that the other was deaf. Then he stood back and listened as the two women screamed at each other.

Residents of San Francisco had not forgotten Derby, and were thrilled that Squibob was again footloose on the muddy alleys of San Francisco. Unlike San Diego's Old Town, San Francisco was a bustling port filled with argonauts, hustlers and pioneers — an exciting mixture for a prankster like Derby. Squibob's celebrated antics spread quickly through San Francisco and are reported in Barry and Patten's *Men and Memories of San Francisco.* Other hilarious incidents were repeated by Mark Twain, a decade later.

Between his pranks, Lt. Derby found time to write for the San Francisco *Herald*, edited by his friend John Nugent. The following article satirized the newly-appointed tax collector and the corrupt spoils system which was rampant during the Gold Rush Era. The article was datelined "The Oriental Hotel," on Bush Street, one door east of Dr. Charles Hitchcock's medical office.

THE ORIENTAL

INAUGURATION OF THE NEW COLLECTOR!

First Printed in the San Francisco Herald, May 25, 1853

PASSING up Montgomery Street yesterday afternoon, between three and four o'clock, my attention was attracted by a little gentleman with a small moustache, who rushed hastily past me, and turning down Commercial Street sought to escape observation by plunging among the crowd of drays that perpetually tangle up Long Wharf. Though slightly lame, he had passed me with a speed that may have been equalled, but for a man of his size could never have been excelled; and his look of frantic terror — his countenance, wild, pallid with apprehension, as I caught for an instant his horror-stricken gaze, I shall never forget. I had turned partly around to watch his flight, when with a sudden shock I was borne hurridly along, and in an instant found myself struggling and plunging in the midst of a mighty crowd who were evidently in hot pursuit. There were old men, young men, and maidens — at least I presume they were maidens, but it was no time for close scrutiny. There were Frenchmen, Englishmen, Chinamen, and every other description of men; gentlemen with spectacles and gentlemen who were spectacles to behold; men with hats and men without hats; an angry sea of moustaches, coattails and hickory shirts, with here and there a dash of foam in the way of a petticoat; and all pouring and rushing down Long Wharf with me in the midst, like a bewildered gander in a mill race.

There was no shouting — a look of stern and gloomy determination sat on the countenance of each individual; and save an occasional muttered ejaculation of "There he goes!" or "I see him!" we rushed on in horrid silence.

A sickly feeling came over me as the conviction that I was in the midst of the far-famed and dreaded Vigilance Committee, settled on my mind. Here I was, borne along with them, an involuntary and unwilling member — I, a life member of the Anti-Capital Punishment Society,* and author of the little work called "Peace, or Directions for the use of the Sword as a Pruning Hook," who never killed a fly in my life — here I was, probably about to countenance, by my presence, the summary execution of the unhappy little culprit with the small moustache, who, for aught I knew to the contrary, might be as immaculate as Brigham Young himself.

What would Brother Greeley say to see me now? But it was no time for reflection. "Onward we drove in dreadful race, pursuers and pursued," over boxes, bales, drays and horses. The Jews screamed and shut their doors as they saw us coming; there was a shower of many-bladed knives, German silver pencils, and impracticable pistols as the showcases flew

---

*Editor's Note — In 1850 Derby was arrested for helping a horse-thief escape lynching by members of the Vigilance Committee.

wildly in the air. It was a dreadful scene. I am not a fleshy man — that is, not particularly fleshy — but an old villain with a bald head and spectacles, punched me in the abdomen; I lost my breath, closed my eyes, and remembered nothing further. On recovering my faculties, I found myself jammed up flat against a sugar box, like a hoe cake, with my head protruding over the top in the most uncomfortable manner, and apparently the weight of the whole crowd (amounting by this time to some six thousand) pressed against me, keeping me inextricably in my position. Here for an instant I caught a glimpse of a Stockton boat just leaving the wharf — then everything was obscured by a sudden shower of something white, and then burst from the mob a deep and melancholy howl, prolonged, terrific, hideous. I wrenched myself violently from the sugar box, and confronted a seedy-looking individual with a battered hat. In his hand he held a crumpled paper, and on his countenance sat the gloom of despair.

"In the name of heaven," I gasped, "what is this?"

"He has escaped," he replied, with a deep groan.

"What had he done?" said I, "who is the criminal?"

"Done," said he of the seedy garments, turning moodily away. "Nothing — *it is the new Collector!!!* He's off to Stockton."

The crowd dispersed; slowly and sadly they all walked off. I looked over the side of the wharf. I am not given to exaggeration. You will believe me when I tell you that the sea was white with letter that had been thrown by that crowd. For miles it was white with them, and far out in the stream her wheels filled with letter paper, her shafts clogged with dissolving wafers, lay the Stockton boat. On her upper deck, in a frenzied agony, danced the pilot, his hand grasping his shattered jaw. An office-seeker had thrown a letter attached to a stone which had dislodged four of his front teeth! As I gazed, the steamer's wheels began to move. At her after-cabin window appeared a nose above a small moustache, a thumb and fingers twinkled for an instant in the sunlight, and she was gone.

I walked up the wharf, and gazed ruefully on my torn clothing and shattered boots, which had suffered much in this struggle of democracy.

"Thank God! Oh, Squibob," said I, "that you are a fool, or what amounts to the same thing in these times — a Whig — and have no offices to dispense, and none to seek for. Verily, the aphorism of Scripture is erroneous: It should read, '*It is equally cursed to give as to receive*'."

I repaired to my room at the Oriental. Passing the chamber of the Collector, I espied within, the chambermaid, an intersting colored person named Nancy. Now I used to have an unworthy prejudice against the colored race; but since reading that delightful and truthful work, "Uncle Stowe's Log," my sympathies are with them, and I have rather encouraged a Platonic attachment for Nancy, which had been engendered between us by numerous acts of civility on my part and amiability on hers. So I naturally stopped to speak to her. *She stood up to her middle in unopened letters*. There must have been on the floor of that room eighteen thousand unopened letters. The monthly mail from the East would be nothing to it.

"Mr. Squibob," said Nancy with a sweet smile, "is you got airy shovel?"

"No, Nancy," said I; "why do you want a shovel?"

"To clar out dese yere letters," said she; "de Collecker said I muss frow dem all away; he don't want no such trash about him."

A thought struck me. I hastened to my room, seized a slop-pail, returned and filled it with letters, opened them, read them, and selected a few, which strike me as peculiarly deserving. If the Collector reads the *Herald* — and I know he "does nothing else" — these must attract his attention, and the object of the writers will be attained. Here they are. Of course, I suppress the dates and signatures; the authors will doubtless be recognized by their peculiar styles, and the time and place at which they were written is quite immaterial.

No. 1

MY DEAR FRIEND — *I assume you will be perfectly surrounded this morning, as usual, by a crowd of heartless office-seekers. I therefore take this method of addressing you. I thank God, I want no office for myself or others. You have known me for years, and have never known me to do a mean or dishonorable action. I saw W—— up on Stockton the other day, and he is very anxious that I should be appointed Inspector of Steamboats. He said that I needed it, and deserved it, and that he hoped you would give it to me; but I told him I was no office-seeker — I should never ask you for any office. He said he would write to you about it. Please write to me as soon as you receive this, care of Parry & Batten.*

Your Affectionate friend

P.S. My friend John Smith, who you know is a true Pierce & King man, is anxious to get the appointment of Weigher and Gauger of Macaroni. He is an excellent fellow, and a true friend of yours. I hope, whether you can spare an Inspectorship for me or not, you will give Smith a chance.

NO. II.

MY DEAR SIR: Allow me to congratulate you on your success in obtaining your wishes. I have called twice to see you, but have not been able to find you in. You were kind enough to assure me, before leaving for Washington, that I might depend upon your friendship. I think it very improbable that I shall be re-nominated. The waterfront Extension project has not been received with that favor that I expected, and what with Roman and the Whigs and that d—d Herald, I feel very doubtful. You will oblige me by retaining in your possession, until after the Convention, the office of —— to the Custom House. I must look about me to command the means of subsistence. I will see you again on this subject.

Very truly yours,

P.S. My young friend, Mr. John Brown, wishes to be made Inspector of Vermicelli. He is a pure Democrat dyed in the wool, and I trust in making your appointments you will not overlook his claims. Brown tells me he considers himself almost a relative of yours. His aunt used to go to school with your father. She frequently writes to him, and always speaks of you with great esteem.

NO. III.

MON AMIE: I ave been ver malade since that I hav arrive, I ver muche thank you for you civilite on la vapor which we come ici, juntos. The peoples here do say to me, you si pued give me the littel offices in you customs house. I wish if si usted ustan you me shall make to be Inspectors de cigarritos. Je l entends muy bien. Come to me see.

Countess de ——

Mister Jose Jones he say wish to be entree clerky. You mucho me oblige by make him do it.

NO. IV.

(The following was evidently dictated by some belligerent old Democrat to an amanuensis, who appears not to have got precisely the ideas intended:)

SIR: I have been a dimocrat of the Jackson School thank God for twenty years. If you sir had been erected to an orifice by the pusillanimous sufferings of the people as I was onst I would have no clam but sir you are appointed by Pierce for whom I voted and King who is dead as Julia's sister and I expectorate the office for which my friends will ask you sir I am a plane man and wont the orifice of Prover and taster of Brandy and wish you write to me at the Niantic where I sick three days and have to write by a young gentleman or come to see me before eleven o'clock when I generally get sick. Yours

P.S. My young man mr. Peter Stokes I request may be made inspector of pipes.

NO. V.

Mr. Colected H——   Detor
Elizer Muggins
fore dosen peaces ....$12..
Receat pament.

MISTER COLECTED My husban Mikel Muggins will wish me write you no matur for abuv if you make him inspector in yore custom hous, he always vote for Jackson and Scott and all the Dimocrats and he vote for Bugler and go for extension the waser works which I like very much. You will much oblige by call and settel this one way or other.

ELIZIR MUGGINS.

P.S. Mike wants Mr. Timothy flaherty, who was sergent in Pirces regiment and held Pirces hoss when he reared and throwed him to be a inspector too hes verry good man.

E.M.

NO. VI.

SIR: I have held for the last four years the appointment of Surveyor of Shellfish in the Custom House, and have done my duty and understand it. I have been a Whig, but never interfered in politics, and should have voted for Pierce — it was my intention — but a friend by mistake gave me a wrong ballot, and I accidentally put it in, having been drinking a little. Dear sir, I hope you will not dismiss me; no man in this city understands a clam as I do, and I shall be very much indebted to you to keep my office for the present though have much finer offers but don't wish at present to accept.

Very respectfully,

P.S. My friend Mr. Thomas Styles wishes to keep his office. Dear sir, he is Inspector of Raccoon Oysters; he is an excellent gentleman, and though they call him a Whig I think dear sir, there is great doubt. I hope you'll keep us both; it's very hard to get good inspectors who understand shell-fish.

So much for today. If any gentleman incited by a laudable curiosity wishes to peruse more of these productions, let him proceed to Telegraph Hill, and on the summit of the tower at the extremity of the starboard yard-arm, in the discharge of his duty will be found, always ready, attentive, courteous and obliging.

SQUIBOB.

LITERARY CONTRIBUTION BOX

San Francisco Herald, June 15, 1853

ON assuming the responsible position of poetical critic for the *Herald,* I applied to my friend Mr. Parry for permission to place in one corner of his San Francisco renowned establishment, a cigar-box, with a perforated sliding cover, for the reception of poetical contributions, a request which that gentleman most urbanely granted. Knowing that "Parry's" was the favorite resort of the wits, literati and savans of the city, I hoped and believed that this enterprise would be crowned with the success that it merited; but either our city poets are unable to find quarters in that establishment, or there is dearth of that description of talent at present; for with the exception of two or three contributions of "old soldiers" and a half-dollar deposited by an inebriated member of the last Legislature, on the representaion of his friends that the box was placed there for the relief of distressed Chinese women, nothing has come of it.

Diurnally, after imbibing my morning glass of bimbo (a temperance drink, composed of three parts of root beer and two of water-gruel, thickened with a little soft squash, and strained through a cane-bottomed chair) I gazed mournfully into that aching void, and turned away to meet the sympathetic glance of Batten, who, being a literary man himself, feels for my disappointment and shakes his head sadly as in reply to my mute inquiry, uttering the significant monosyllable "Nix."

But this morning my exertions were rewarded: "I had a bite." In my box I found the following contribution, and feeling delighted at my success, and to encourage others who may dread criticism, I shall publish it without remark or annotation, merely premising that I know nothing whatever of M.W., but that he appears to be a worthy and impulsive young fellow, who, having become possessed of five dollars, invested it very properly in the purchase of a ticket at the American Theatre, where he incontinently fell in love with Mrs. Heald (as possibly others may have done before him and where he hastily "threw off" the following lines, written doubtless on the back of a playbill, immediately after the conclusion of the Spider Dance, when he probably found himself in a sweet state, compounded of love, excitement and perspiration, caused by a great physical exertion, in producing the *encore*. Here it is:

TO LOLA MONTES.

FAIR LOLA!
I cannot believe, as I gaze on thy face,
And into thy soul-speaking eye,
There rests in thy bosom one lingering trace
Of a spirit the world should decry.
No, Lola, no!

I read in those eyes, and on that clear brow,
A Spirit — a Will — it is true;
I trace there a Soul — kind, loving, e'en now;
But it is not a wanton I view;
No, Lola, no!

I will not believe thee cold, heartless and vain!
Man's victim thou ever hast been!
With thee rests the sorrow, on thee hangs the chain,
Then on thee should the world cast the sin?
No, Lola, no.

M.W."

Now isn't this — but I promised not to criticise. Try it again, M.W. — you'll do! Winn, who is looking over my shoulder, and is a connoisseur in the description of poetry, says it is very fair — but he will persist in inquiring "what chain is alluded to in the last line but one?" He thinks "there is a link wanting there to complete the connection."

But never mind this, M.W.; he would be glad enough to reward you liberally for a similar laudatory of buckwheat cakes and golden syrup. Don't be disheartened! Just you go on and fill the cigar box, confident of deserving the "smiles" of Parry, the "cheer" of Batten, and the appreciation, with a "first-rate notice," of your admiring

SQUIBOB.

During the Gold Rush Period, the California political scene was dominated by the Democratic Party, and bribery, influence peddling, and a corrupt spoils system was rampant. Although he is barely remembered today, one of the first governors of California was Colonel Bigler, who wielded immense power during his two terms as governor. In fact, for a brief moment in Gold Rush history, Lake Tahoe was named in his honor.

In politics, Derby was a Whig, then known as the Reform Party. When the incumbent Bigler ran for Governor in 1853, Squibob's letters to the San Francisco *Herald* mocking Bigler became so popular that Hull, the Whig Campaign manager, offered a hundred dollars apiece for the Squibob letters for campaign purposes.

Squibob's jokes were **so** good that a rival political satirist appropriated the name and soon a second "Squibob" was in the field and writing for the *Herald's* competitor, *The Evening Journal.*

Governor John Bigler
Courtesy San Francisco Public Library

Derby was outraged at the theft of the humorous nickname he had used since West Point. At first he tried to silence the "malicious" rival with a series of letters to the *Evening Journal.* When this failed to silence the imposter, Derby committed "literary suicide" in the following humorous letter to the San Francisco *Herald.*

A Very
Mournful
Chapter

Death and Spirit Resurrection
Of Squibob

First printed in the San Francisco Herald, June 16, 1853

SAN FRANCISCO, **June 15, 1853**. It becomes my melancholy duty to inform you of the decease, under most painful circumstances, of your friend and contributor, the unfortunate "Squibob." It has been evident to the public for some days past that his faculties were becoming much impaired, and his friends had noticed, with regret, growing evidences of imbecility, evinced by a disposition to make unnecessary and inappropriate puns, and a tendency to ridicule the Board of Aldermen, the code of duelling, and other equally serious subjects and sacred institutions. Hopes were still entertained of his rallying, and many believed that he would yet be spared to us; but, on the 13th instant, he was seized with a violent attack of the *Evening Journal* — a species of intermittent epidemic which made its appearance regularly at four o'clock each afternoon, and under the influence of which he rapidly sunk. He sent for me late yesterday evening, and I had the mournful satisfaction of being with him in his last moments, and of closing one of his eyes. I say one of his eyes, for the other persisted in remaining partly open, and his interesting countenance, even in death, preserves that ineffable wink of intelligence which so eminently characterized him while among the living.

I found him suffering much from physical and mental prostration, but evidently well aware of his approaching end, and calm and resigned in the contemplation of that event. Some idea may be formed of his condition "from a remark that he made:"

"I sent to the cook for a *broiled* pork chop," he feebly articulated, "and he sent me a *fried* one. It is satisfactory, in one's last moments, thus to receive the consolations of religion from a *San Francisco Friar.*"

I could not resist an expression of horror at this sad evidence of the alarmingly low state to which he had been brought. He smiled sadly, and said with ineffable sweetness, "Never mind — it's better so. My friends have all advised me to die, and it is my safest course. If I had continued in the papers, some bellicose individual would have 'called me *out*,' and the *Herald* would have been 'rifled of its sweets.'"

He was here seized with an alarming paroxysm, during which his hands were extended in a right line from the tip of his nose, the fingers separated and "twiddling" (if I may be allowed the expression) in a convulsive manner.

On recovering, his eye fell on a copy of the *Evening Journal.* He shuddered, and muttering in an incoherent manner, "I am done Brown," turned away.

I then gave him a glass of "Bimbo," which appeared to arouse his energies, and he requested that his daguerreotype of "Green," in his great character of Sir Harcourt Courtly, might be shown him. As I held before him the representation of that artist, a barrel organ in the street below struck up his favorite tune, "The Low-Backed Car." As the well-known sound struck his ear, a light spread over his countenance. Sitting up in bed, he seized the miniature and clasped it to his breast.

"Where is M.W.?" he screamed. "Give it to me quick!!"

I hastily handed him yesterday's *Herald*. His eye fell on the lines. Gazing alternately on them and the miniature, and eagerly listening to the organ — "Poetry! Music! And the Drama!" he exclaimed.

"Farewell! Farewell, for ever!"

The light passed from his visage, his eye glazed, and falling back upon his pillow, his gentle spirit passed away without a struggle.

I had left the room to give directions to the weeping Nancy, with reference to the disposal of the body, when returning, judge to my surprise at finding him sitting up in bed.

"Look here, old fellow," said he, "By George! I quite forgot my last words —*'This is the last of earth! — I still live!! — I WISH THE CONSTITUTION TO BE RESERVED!!! — HERE'S LUCK!!!!'"*

Then lying down, and closing one eye, with a wink, the intense meaning of which beggars all description, he expired — this time "positively without reserve."

P.S. The funeral ceremonies will take place tomorrow at 11 o'clock at "Patty and Barren's," when the public generally are invited to attend (with rifles). The "Tangarees" (of which association the deceased was a member) and the "Moral Reform Society," will form around the bier (*lager*) and accompany the body to its last resting place.

Winn is now busily engaged in the melancholy duty of modelling his features in soft gingerbread. A copy of the bust in candy he promises shall be sent to the offices of the *Herald* and the *Evening Journal*.

A Spiritual Medium (one of the tipping ones) has just been experimenting in the room with the remains. The following questions were put, eliciting the following answers:

QUESTION. "Is the spirit of Squibob present?"

ANSWER. "Slightually."

QUESTION. "Are you happy?"

ANSWER. "Rather."

The Spirit here asked, through the Medium, the following question:

"Are the public generally glad I am dead?"

A regard for veracity compelled every person in the room to reply: "Very!"

When the Table on which the experiments were being conducted was violently capsized and the remains sitting up in bed threw a boot at the Medium —which broke up the meeting — the Medium very properly remarked that "it would be bootless to prosecute the inquiry further."

Should anything further of interest transpire, I will take much pleasure in informing you.

Yours respectfully,

SKEWBALL

The subject of the following satire was the San Francisco Ladies' Protection and Relief Society, which was founded during the summer of 1853 by the wives of San Francisco's influential citizens. It was Derby's first published article using his new *nom de plume* —"JOHN PHOENIX." Derby no doubt borrowed the pseudonym from youthful San Francisco which had chosen the magical bird *Phoenix* as its heraldic emblem. Like the city that had risen from the ashes of numerous fires, so "Squibob" had arisen again.

The Ladies' Relief Society

First Printed in the Alta California, July 1853

SAN FRANCISCO, **July 12, 1853**. Learning that a meeting of the "Ladies' Relief Society" was to be held this morning at Pine Church, on Baptist Street, your Reporter, actuated by a desire to discharge his duty to the public by collecting valuable information, and incited by a laudable curiosity to ascertain what on earth the ladies desired to be relieved from (on which last point he obtained the most complete satisfaction, as will appear) repaired to that sacred edifice and ensconsing himself in a pew conveniently situated near the door, in case of a sudden retreat becoming expedient, patiently awaited the commencement of the proceedings.

At half past nine a.m. precisely, as I ascertained by reference to the magnificent silver watch, valued at $18, which I did **not** draw in Tobin and Duncan's grand raffle yesterday, but which "on the contrary, quite the reverse," was bestowed upon me by my deceased Grandmother (excuse the digression); I am approaching a painful subject and like to do it gradually, the ladies began to assemble in their beauty and, I regret to add, their strength. From the somewhat inconvenient position which, from motives of delicacy and a desire to avoid the appearance of intrusion, I had assumed on the floor of the pew, I counted fifty-two of the "sweeteners of our cup of human happiness," of every age, figure and appearance. There was the maid of blushing sixteen, and there was the widow of sixty, dressed in all imaginable styles of color — white hats, red shawls, chip bonnets, green aprons, and pink-colored boots.

The Pine Church looked like a conservatory, and as I lay *perdue*, like an innocent (green) snake among the flowers listening to the merry laugh and innocent playful gurglings of delight that fell from their hundred and four lips:

"How d'do, dear?"

"My, what a love of a bonnet!"

"What did you draw, Fanny?"

"Is Lizzy going to marry that fellow?"

As the town clock struck ten, the doors were closed, and a lady of mature age and benign though unyielding expression (I do you justice, Madam, though), ascended the steps of the pulpit, and taking from the desk of a fireman's speaking trumpet that laid thereon, she smote an awful blow upon a copy of the scared scriptures and vociferated through the brazen instrument, "*Order!*"

Conversation ceased. Laughter was hushed, and with the exception of an irrepressible murmur and a subdued snicker from your reporter, as some charming being exclaimed, *sotto voce*, "don't pinch me," silence reigned profound.

"Ladies," said the President, "you are aware of the object of this meeting. Tied down by the absurd prejudices of society; trammelled by the shackles of custom and unworthy suspicion; we have found it necessary to form ourselves into a society, where, free from the intrusion of execrable man; aloof from his jealous scrutiny, whether as father, brother, or that still more objectionable character of husband, we may throw off restraint, exert our natural liberty, and seek relief from the tedious and odious routine of duty imposed upon us in our daily walk of life. Any motion is in order."

At this instant, while my wondering gaze was attracted by an elderly female in a Tuscan bonnet amd green veil* who, drawing a black pint bottle from the pocket of her dress, proceeded to take a "snifter" therefrom, with vast apparent satisfaction, and then tendered it to the lady that sat next (a sweet little thing in a Dunstable, with cherry-colored ribbons) a lady rose and said:

"Mrs. President, I move that a committee of one be appointed to send a servant to Batty and Parrens for fifty-two *brandy smashes.*"

A thrill of horror ran through my veins; I rose mechanically to my feet; exclaimed "gracious goodness!" and fell, in a fainting condition, against the back of the pew. It was my Susan! You remember the instant that intervenes between the flash of the lightning and the ensuing thunder clap — for an instant there was silence, dead silence, you might have heard a paper of pins fall — then "at once there rose so wild a yell."

"A man! A man!" they cried, and a scene of hubbub and confusion ensued that beggars description. The venerable female in the Tuscan shyed the pint bottle at my head — the little thing in the Dunstable gave me a back-handed wipe with a parasol, and for an instant my life was in positive danger

* Editor's Note — One of the founders the Ladies' Relief Society was Mrs. Hitchcock, wife of Derby's friend Dr. Charles Hitchcock. She is unkindly described by Derby in this satire as the "elderly female in a Tuscan bonnet and green veil."

from the shower of fans, hymn books and other missiles that fell around me.

"Put him out, Martha," said an old lady to a lovely being in a blue dress in an adjacent pew.

"I shan't," was the reply, "I haven't been introduced to him."

"Wretched creature," said the President in an awful voice,"who are you?"

"Reporter for the *Alta*," rose to my throat, but my lips refused their utterance.

"What do you want?" she continued.

"I want to go home," I feebly articulated.

"Put him out!" she rejoined, and before I could think, much less expostulate, I was pounced upon by two strong-minded women, and found myself walking rapidly down Baptist Street, with the impression of a number three gaiter boot on my clothing about ten inches below the two ornamental buttons upon the small of my back. From this latter circumstance, I have formed the impression that the little thing with the Dunstable and cherry-colored ribbons assisted at my elimination.

And now, Mr. Editor, what are we to think of this? Does it not give rise to very serious reflections that a society should exist in our very midst of so nefarious — but indignation is useless. "I cannot do justice to the subject."

Ruffled in disposition, wounded to the heart in the best and most sacred feelings of my common nature, I can only subscribe myself,

Your outraged Reporter,

PHOENIX

"SQUIBOB" IN LOVE

While he waited for the War Department's answer on the San Diego River proposal, Derby roamed the alleys of San Francisco. He was treated like a celebrity, and according to Barry and Patten, San Franciscans would sometimes stop just to listen to his celebrated wit. Despite his weight, the portly lieutenant was a handsome man with dark hair and a round, bearded face. But it was Derby's sparkling eyes and magical smile that captured the heart of twenty-four-year-old Mary Angeline Coons, who had just arrived in San Francisco with her widowed mother from St. Louis, Missouri. After being introduced by the Hitchcocks in early summer 1853, Mary and George fell madly in love.

The Coons family, however, objected to Mary's marriage to a second lieutenant whose erratic, flippant behavior had infuriated his superiors. It didn't matter that Derby had descended from a distinguished family in Salem. George's father, John Barton Derby, had deserted his family to write poetry and was spending the family fortune self-publishing. With his recently published "Squibob" articles, it appeared that George Derby was headed towards the same "madness."

With his romantic problems, Derby was almost relieved to learn that the War Department had reached a decision on the San Diego River project. The lieutenant boarded a ship for San Diego in August and swore he would not return to San Francisco until Mary Coons' mother and brother had left the city.

PHOENIX Takes Affectionate Leave of San Francisco

First printed in the Alta California, August 21, 1853

SAN DIEGO, **August 10, 1853**. It was about 7 1/2 A.M. on the first day of this present month of August that I awakened from a very pleasant dream in the great city of San Francisco to the very unpleasant conviction that it was a damp and disagreeable morning and that my presence was particularly required in the small city of San Diego. So, having shaken hands with Frink, taken an affectionate leave of the chambermaid, and lastly, devoured a beefsteak at the Branch of Alden which viand, in perfect keeping with the weather was both cold and raw, I shouldered my cane with a carpet bag suspended at each end, "a la Chinois," and left the Tehama House without "one lingering hope or fond regret."

When a man is going down everybody lends him a kick, an aphorism which I came very near realizing in my own proper person for as I went on my way down Long Wharf I accidentally grazed a mule who, being in an evil frame of mind and harnessed to a dray, might be considered as passionately attached to that conveyance. This interesting animal, fancying from my appearance that I was "going down" lent me a kick which, had his legs been two inches longer, would have put a stop to my correspondence forever. As it was I escaped and hurried on down the wharf thinking with a shudder on the mysterious prophecy of my friend little Miss B., who had told me I was "sure to be kicked" before I left San Francisco, and wondering if she was really "among the prophets."

The *Northerner*, like the steamboat runners, was *lying* at the end of the wharf, blowing off steam, and as usual when a steamer is about to leave for Panama, a great crowd surrounded her. What made them all get up so early? Out of the three or four hundred people on the end of that wharf I don't believe fifty had friends that were about to sail. No! They love to look upon a steamer leaving. It brings to their minds recollections of the dear ones at home to whom she is speeding with fond tidings, and they love to gaze and wish to Heaven they were going in her. The usual mob of noisy fruit venders encompassed the gangway plank; green pears they sold to greener purchasers; apples also, whereof everything but the shape of an apple had long since departed, and oranges — the recollection of one of which doth to this day abide in me and set my teeth on edge. But high above their din, the roar of the steamer and the murmuring of the crowd rang the shrill cry of the newsboy in his unknown tongue:

"Here's the Alteruldniguntimes Heup!"

I stepped across the plank and found myself in the presence of three fine bullocks. How fat and sleek they looked; uneasy though, as if they smelled mischief in the wind.

A tall gaunt specimen of Pike County humanity stood regarding them approvingly, his head thrown slightly back to get their points to better advantage. It was the tomb gazing on its victim. As I paused for a moment to look at the picture, Pike yawned fearfully, his head opening like the top of an old-fashioned fall-back chaise. The nearest bullock, turning, caught his eye. I thought the unhappy animal shuddered and nudged his companion, as who should say, "Ye living, come and view the grave where you shall shortly lie."

It was quite a touching little scene. On deck all was bustle and excitement. The sailors, apparently in the last extremity of physical suffering, judging from their agonized cries, were heaving away at mysterious ropes. The mate, Mr. Dall, was engaged in busy, not tender dalliance with the breast lines, while Burns the purser exhibited an activity and good nature only to be accounted for by the supposition that he had eaten two boxes of Russia salve (which is good for Burns — see your advertising columns) for his breakfast.

As the last line fell from the dock and our noble steamer with a mighty throb and deep sigh, at bidding *adieu* to San Francisco, swung slowly round, the passengers crowded to the side to exchange a farewell salutation with their friends and acquaintances.

"Goodbye, Jones,"

"Goodbye, Brown."

"God bless you old fellow, take care of yourself!" they shouted.

Not seeing anyone that I knew, and fearing the passengers might think I had no friends, I shouted "Goodbye, Muggins," and had the satisfaction of having a shabby man, much inebriated, reply as he swung his rimless hat, "Goodbye, my brother."

Not particularly elated at this recognition, I tried again with "Goodbye, Colonel," whereat thirty-four respectable gentlemen took off their hats, and I got down from the position that I had occupied on a camp stool, with much dignity, inwardly wondering whether my friends were all aides to Bigler, in which case their elevated rank and affection for me would both be satisfactorily accounted for.

Away we sped down the bay, the captain standing on the wheelhouse directing our course.

"Port, Port a little, Port," he shouted.

"What's he a-calling for?" inquiring a youth of good-natured but unmistakable verdancy of appearance, of me.

"Port wine," said I, "and the storekeeper don't hear him. You'd better take him up some."

"I will," said Innocence, "I've got a bottle of first rate in my state room."

And he did, but soon returned with a particularly crest-fallen and sheepish appearance.

"Well, what did he say to you?" inquired I.

"Pointed at the notice on that tin," said the poor fellow."'Passengers not allowed on the wheelhouse.' *He* is, though, ain't he?" added my friend with a faint attempt at a smile as the captain in an awful voice shouted, "Starboard!"

"Is what?" said I.

"Loud on the wheel-house!"

Good God! I went below.

At 9 o'clock in the evening we arrived at Monterey, where our modest salute was answered by the thundering response of a 24-pounder from the fort. This useful defensive work, which mounts some twenty heavy guns and contains quarters for a regiment, was built in 1848 by Halleck, Peachy & Billings. It is now used as a hermitage by a lonely officer of the U.S. Army. The people of Monterey have a wild legend concerning this desolate recluse. I was told that he passes the whole of his time in sleep, never by any chance getting out of bed until he hears the gun of a steamer, when he rushes forth in his shirt, fires off a 24-pounder, sponges and reloads it, takes a drink and turns in again. They never have seen him. It's only by his *semi-monthly reports* they know of his existence.

"Well," said I to my informant, a bustling little fellow named Bootjacks who came off on board with us, "suppose some day a steamer should arrive and he should not return her gun?"

"Well sir," replied Bookjacks with a quaint smile, "we should conclude that he was either dead, *or out of powder.*"

Logical deduction this, and a rather curious story. Altogether, how I should like to see him!

Bootjacks kindly presented me with the following state of the markets etc. in Monterey, which will give you a better idea of the large business and commercial prosperity of that flourishing city than anything that I can write on those subjects.

MONTEREY MARKETS

The arrival of a stranger by the *Major Tompkins* from San Francisco during the past week, with specie to the amount of $4.87 1/2, most of which has been put in circulation, has produced an unprecedented activity among our businessmen. Confidence is in a great measure restored and our merchants have had no reason to complain of want of occupation. The following is the state of our market, for the principal articles of domestic consumption:

FLOUR: Twenty-five pounds, imported by Boston & Co., per *Major Tompkins*, still in first hands; flour in small quantities is jobbing readily at 15 & 18 cents per lb. We notice sales of 10 lb by Boston & Co., to Judge Merritt, on private terms.

PORK: The half bbl. imported by Col. Russell in March last, is nearly all in the hands of jobbers; sales of 4 lb. at $1, half cash; remainder in note at 4 months. A half bbl. expected by Bootjack Co., early in September, will overstock the market.

CANDY: Sales of 6 sticks by Boston & Co. to purser of *Major Tompkins* on private terms; the market has a downward tendency; candy is jobbing in sticks at 6 & 8 cents.

POTATOES: We notice arrival of 10 lbs from the *Santa Cruz*; no sales.

DRY GOODS: Sales of two cotton pocket hdkfs. by McKinley & Co. at 62 1/2 & 75 cents; endorsed note at 6 months.

Lively place this. Thank Heaven my lot is not cast there — it was once, but the people sold it for taxes. Having taken on board the U.S. mail, containing one letter (which I believe must have been the resignation of the Collector), our noble steamer bore away to the southward.

Four bells tinkled from the little bell aft; four bells chimed from its deep-toned brother foreward; and being of a retiring disposition, I retired.

Sketched by J. W. Revere U. S. N.

MONTEREY

· O R I Z A B A ·
Wooden Side-Wheel Steamer, 1355 tons, 246' x 35' x 16.4',
oak frames, chestnut planking, built by Jacob A. Westervelt,
N.Y. 1854 Cost $240,000. Vertical beam engine 65" x 11, by
Morgan Iron Works, N.Y. Dismantled San Francisco 1887.

Scale in feet
SAN DIEGO HISTORICAL SOCIETY — 1959

Courtesy The San Diego Historical Society

PHOENIX AT SEA

First printed in the Alta California, August 23, 1853

BRIGHT and beautiful rose the sun from out the calm blue
sea, its early rays gleaming on the snow-white decks of
the *Northerner*, and "gliding refined gold" as they penetrated
the state room "A," and lingering, played among the tresses
of the slumbering McAuburn. It was a lovely morning, "the
winds were all hushed and the waters at rest," and no sound
was heard but the throbbing of the engine and the splash of
the paddle wheels as the gallant old *Northerner* sped on her
way "tracking the trackless sea."

Two sailors engaged in their morning devotions with the
holy stones near my room amused me not a little. One of them,
either accidentally or with "malice prepense," threw a bucket
of water against the bulwark which *ricocheting*, struck the
other on his dorsal extremity as he leaned to his work, making
that portion of his frame exceedingly damp and him exceedingly angry.

"You just try that again — your soul," exclaimed the offended one, "and I'll slap your chops for you."

"Oh, yes you will," sarcastically rejoined he with the water bucket; "I've heerd of you afore! *You're old chop-slapper's son, ain'y you? Father went round slapping people's chops, didn't he?*"

Then followed a short fight in which, as might have been expected, "Old chop-slapper's son" got rather the worst of it.

There was no excuse for being sick that morning so our passengers, still pale but with cheerful hope depicted in their countenances, soon began to throng the deck, cigars were again brought into requisition and we had an opportunity of ascertaining whether there was any Bourbon among us.

A capital set of fellows they were. There was Moore, and Parker, and Bowers (one of Joe Bowers' boys), and Sarsaparilla, Meade, and Freeman; which last mentioned gentlemen, so amusing were they, appeared to be travelling *expressly* to entertain us. And there were no ladies, which to me was a blessed dispensation.

> *Oh, woman! in our hours of ease*
> *Uncertain, coy, and hard to please;*
> *When pain and anguish wring the brow,*
> *A ministering angel thou.*

Certainly. But at sea, Woman, you are decidedly disagreeable. In the first place you generally bring babies with you, which are a crying evil, and then you have to have the best stateroom and the first seat at the table, and monopolize the captain's attention and his room, and you make remarks to one another about us and our cigars and profanity, and accuse us of singing rowdy songs, and you generally wind up by doing some scandalous thing yourself, when half of us take your part and the other half don't, and we get all together by the ears a pretty state of affair ensues. No, woman! Thou are agreeable enough on shore, if taken homeopathically, but on a steamer you are a decided nuisance.

We had a glorious day aboard the old *Northerner*; we played whist and sang songs and told stories, many of which were coeval with our ancient school-lessons, and like them came very easily, going over the second time. Many drank strong waters and becoming mopsed thereon, toasted "the girls we left behind us," whereat one, who, being a temperance man, had guzzled soda-water until his eyes seemed to *pop* from his head, pondered deeply, sighed, and said nothing.

And so we laughed, and sang, and played, and whiskied, and soda-watered through the day. And fast the old *Northerner* rolled on. And at night the Captain gave us a grand game supper in his room at which game we played not, but went at it in sober earnest. And then there were more songs (the same ones, though, and the same stories too, over again), and some speechifying, and much fun until at eight bells we separated; some shouting, some laughing, some crying (but not with sorrow), but all extremely happy as we turned in.

But before I sought state-room "A" that night, I executed a small scheme for insuring undisturbed repose, which I had resolved in my mind during the day and which met with most brilliant success, as you shall hear.

You remember the two snobs that every night, in the pursuit of exercise under difficulties walk up and down on the deck, arm in arm, right over your state-room. You remember how, when just as you are getting into your first doze, they commence — tramp! tramp! tramp! right over your head. Then you "hear them fainter, fainter still." You listen in horrible dread of their return, nourishing the while a feeble-minded hope that they may have gone below when — horror! Here they come louder, louder, til: Tramp! Tramp! Tramp! They go over your head again.

And with rage in your heart, at the conviction that sleep is impossible, you sit up in bed and despairingly light an unnecessary cigar.

They were on board the *Northerner*, and the night before had aroused my indignation to that strong pitch that I had determined on their downfall. So, before retiring I proceeded to the upper deck and there did I quietly attach a small cord to the stanchions, which stretching across about six inches from the planking, formed what in maritime matters is known as a "booby trap."

This done, I repaired to my room, turned in and calmly awaited the result. In ten minutes they came. I heard them laughing together as they mounted the ladder. Then they commenced the exercise.

Louder. Louder. Tramp! Tramp! Tramp!

Thump! (a double-barrelled thump).

Down they came together. Oh, what a fall was there, my countrymen.

Two deep groans were elicited, and then followed by what, if published, would make two closely-printed royal octavo pages of profanity. I heard them d—n the soul of the man that did it. It was *my* soul that they alluded to, but I cared not. I lay there chuckling. "They called, but I answered not again;" and when at length they limped away, their loud profanity subdued to a blasphemous growl, I turned over in a sweet frame of mind and falling instantaneously asleep, dreamed a dream, a happy dream of "home and thee" — Susan Ann Jane!

The next morning bright and early, the Coronados hove in sight, and at 10 o'clock we rounded Point Loma and ran alongside the coal hulk *Clarissa Andrews* at the Playa of San Diego — just forty-nine hours from San Francisco.

The captain (he is the crew also) of the *Clarissa Andrews*, the gallant Bogart, stood on her rail steady to catch our flying line, and in a few moments we were secured alongside — our engine motionless and my journey ended.

It was with no small regret that I bade *adieu* to our merry passengers and our glorious captain. Noble fellow! I don't wonder enthusiastic passengers get up subscriptions and make speeches and present plate and trumpets, and what not to such men. It's very natural.

A good captain is sure to have a good ship; a voyage with him becomes an agreeable matter. He makes his passengers happy and they very naturally fall in love with him and seek some method of displaying their attachment and "trumpeting his praise abroad."

Our captain was one of this sort; kind, courteous and obliging and "every inch a sailor." He is as much beloved and respected by his passengers as Dick Whiting of the *California* (who to my mind is the *ne plus ultra* of steamboat men), and when I say that the first letter of his name is Isham, I'm sure everybody that ever travelled with him will agree with me.

The *Northerner*, too, is a splendid and most comfortable ship. Which of the Pacific mailboats is not, however? And this subject brings to my mind a little circumstance which took place the day before I left San Francisco.

A shabby-genteel individual with a pale face, in the center of which shone a purple nose that couldn't be beat (though it resembled the vegetable of that name) called on me, and drawing from his coat-tail pocket with an air of mystery a voluminous manuscript, spread it solemnly before me and requested my signature. It was a petition to Congress — or Mr. Pierce, or Mr. John Bigler, or somebody — to transfer the contract for carrying the mails from the "Pacific Company" to "Vanderbilt's Line," and was signed by Brown & Co., Jones & Co., Smith & Brothers, Noakes, Stiles & Thompson, and ever so many more responsible firms, whereof I recognized but one which deals in candy nightly at the corner of Commercial and Montgomery Streets and pays no taxes, and whose correspondence with the Eastern States I suspect is not large.

I love to sign my name. It is a weakness that most modest men have. I love to write it, and cut it, and scratch it in steeples and monuments and other places of public resort. Most men do. It looks pretty, passes away time, perpetuates their memory among posterity, and *costs nothing*. I frequently buy something that I don't want at all, just for the pleasure of signing my name to a check (I bought a ridiculous buggy the other day for no other reason that I can imagine). But I had no inclination to append my autograph to *that* petition and declined, positively and peremptorily — declined.

My friend with the nose rolled up his eyes and rolled up his paper, pocketed it, and was about to withdraw.

"Stop!" said I, as a vivid recollection flashed across my mind. "What are you going about with that paper for? Didn't I see you a few months ago marching down the street at the head of a long progression bearing a big banner with 'Vanderbilt's Death Line!' in great letters thereon, and giving vent to all sorts of scurrility against the Nicaragua route?"

The red nose grew redder as he muttered something about "a man's being obliged to get a living," and he retired.

I saw him go and get his boots blacked by a Frenchman right opposite, give him a quarter and get him to sign his name, which that exile did and thought it was a receipt for the money. And I laughed heartily. But it is no laughing matter.

Having taken leave of all on board the dear old *Northerner*, and shaken hands twice all round, during which process the mate sang out, "Bare a hand there," and I mechanically took off my glove.

McAuburn and I were transported to the shore where, while waiting for a wagon to take us to the town of San Diego, we stopped at the little public house of the Playa, kept by a civil fellow named Donahoo, whom the Spaniards here, judging from his name (*Don't know who*) believe to be the son of old "*Quien Sabe*" himself. What befell us there and thereafter I will shortly inform you.

SQUIBOB — *The mortal remains of this celebrated Patriot and Philantropist were brought down from San Francisco on the Steamer Oregon last week, for interment in the family vault. Domestic duties prevented our being present at the funeral obsequies, but we have been informed that the ceremonies were very impressive. As the cortege passed through the main plaza in front of our office, our foreman, assisted by "Johnny" and General Curry, mustered the Herald forces in a line on the front gallery, and struck up that mournful and touching hymn, commencing:*

> *Mit A tuden Links and a hyden schapps*
> *Widde, Widde, Winktum rum.*

As a man, Squibob was that admirable and remarkable specimen of nature's handiwork — an honest, generous, kindhearted gentleman. As a friend, he was sincere and disinterested. In all the relations of life, he was scrupulous in the discharge of his various duties — And when at last he felt it necessary to sacrifice his existence to perpetuate that of the Evening Journal, he met his fate like a true man, and went off as quiet as a lamb.

PHOENIX IN SAN DIEGO

First printed in the Alta California, August 26, 1853

THE BAY of San Diego is shaped like a boot, the leg forming the entrance to the sea and the toe, extending some
twelve miles inland at right angles to it, as a matter of course,
points southward to the latter end of Mexico, from which it is
distant at present precisely three miles!

The three villages then, which go to make up the great city
of San Diego, are the Playa, Old Town, and New Town, or
"Davis's Folly." At the Playa there are but few buildings at
present and these are not remarkable for size or architectural
beauty of design. A long, low, one-storied tenement, near the
base of the hills, once occupied by rollicking Captain
Magruder and the officers under his command, is now the
place where Judge Witherby, like Matthew, patiently "sits at
the receipt of customs." But few *customers* appear, for with
the exception of the mail steamers once a fortnight, and the
Goliah and *Ohio,* two little coasting steamers that wheeze in

and out once or twice a month, the calm waters of San Diego Bay remain unruffled by keel or cutwater from one year's end to another. Such a thing as a foreign bottom has never made its appearance to gladden the Collector's heart; in this respect, the harbour has indeed proved bottomless. Two crazy old hulks riding at anchor and the barge *Clarissa Andrews* (filled with coal for M.S.S. Co. wherein dwells Captain Bogart, like a second Robinson Crusoe with a man Friday, who is mate, cook, steward and all hands, make up the amount of shipping at the Playa.

Then there is the Ocean House (that's Donahoe's) and a store marked Gardiner & Bleeker, the inside of which nothing could be bleeker for there's nothing in it, and an odd-looking little building on stilts out in the water where a savant named Sabot, in the employ of the U.S. Engineers, makes mysterious observations on the tide. These with three other small unoccupied buildings, a fence and a graveyard constitute all the "improvements" that have been made at the Playa. The ruins of two old hide-houses, immortalized by Dana in his *Two Years Before the Mast*, are still standing, one bearing the weather-beaten name of Tasso. We examined these houses and got well bitten by fleas for our trouble.

We also examined the other great curiosity of the Playa — a natural one — being a cleft in the adjacent hills some hundred feet in depth with a smooth, hard floor of white sand and its walls of indurated clay, perforated with cavities wherein dwell countless numbers of great white owls from which Captain Bogart calls it "Owldom."

Through the cleft we marched into the bowels of the land without impediment for nearly half a mile when, being brought to a standstill by a high, smooth wall, McAuburn did proceed to carve thereon a name. But as he laid out his work on too extensive a scale, the letters being about three feet in length — though he worked with amazing energy — he got no farther than this: **JO**, when his knife broke and the inscription remained incomplete.

Whether, therefore, it was intended to perpetuate to posterity the memory of the great Joseph Bowers, or one of his girls, we may never know, as Mac showed no disposition to be communicative and indeed requested me to "dry up," when I questioned him on the subject.

From the present appearances one would be little disposed to imagine that the playa in five or six years might become a city of the size of Louisville, with brick buildings, paved streets, gas lights, theatres, gambling houses, *and so forth*. It is not at all improbable, however, should the great Pacific Railroad terminate at San Diego, an event with the range of probability, the Playa must be the depot, and as such will become a point of great importance. The landholders about here are well aware of this fact and consequently affix already incredible prices to very unprepossessing pieces of land. Lots of one hundred and fifty front, not situated in particularly eligible places either, have been sold within the last few weeks for five hundred dollars apiece. *"De gustibus,"* & Co. At present I confess I should prefer the money to the real estate.

While at the Playa I had the pleasure of forming an acquaintance with the Pilot, Captain Wm. G. Oliver, as noble a specimen of a sailor as you would wish to see. He was a lieutenant in the Texas navy, under the celebrated Moore, and told me many yarns concerning that gallant commander. Great injustice, I think, has been done in not giving to these officers the rank to which they are entitled in our service. Captain Oliver would do honor to any navy in the world for besides being a thorough seaman, he is an accomplished and agreeable gentleman.

Leaving the Playa in a wagon drawn by two wild mules, driven at the top of their speed by the intrepid Donaho, Mac and I were whirled over a hard road, smooth and even as a ballroom floor, on our way to "Old Town." Five miles from the "Playa" we passed the estate of the Hon. John Hays, County Judge of San Diego, an old Texian and a most amiable gentleman. The judge has a fine farm of eighty or one hundred acres under high cultivation, and what few gentlemen in California can boast of — a private fish pond! He has enclosed some twenty acres of the flats near his residence, having a small outlet with a net attached, from which he daily makes a haul almost equalling the miraculous draught on the Lake Gennesaret.

The old town of San Diego is pleasantly situated on the left bank of the little river that bears its name. It contains perhaps a hundred houses, some of wood, but mostly of the "Adoban" or "Grecian" order of architecture. A small Plaza forms the center of the town, one side of which is occupied by a little *adobe* building used as a courtroom, the "Colorado House," a wooden structure, whereof the second story is occupied by the San Diego *Herald,* as a vast sign bearing that legend informed us, and the Exchange, a hostelry, at which we stopped. This establishment is kept by Hoof (familiarly known as Johnny, but whom I once christened *Cloven*) and Tibbetts, who is also called *Two Bitts*, in honorable distinction from an unworthy partner he once had, who obtained unenviable notoriety as *"Picayune Smith."*

On entering we found ourselves in a large bar and billiard room fitted up with customary pictures and mirrors. Here I saw Lieut. Derby, of the Topographical Engineers, an elderly gentleman of emaciated appearance and serious cast of features. Constant study and unremitting attention to his laborious duties have reduced him almost to a skeleton, but there are not wanting those who say that an unrequited attachment in his early days is the cause of his care-worn appearance. He was sent out from Washington some months since "to dam the San Diego River," and he informed me with a deep sigh and melancholy smile that he had done it (mentally) several times since his arrival.

Here, also, I made the acquaintance of Squire Moon, a jovial middle-aged gentleman from the State of Georgia who replied to my inquiries concerning his health that he was "as fine as silk, but not half so well beliked by the ladies."

After partaking of supper, which meal was served up in the rear of the billiard room *al fresco* from a clothless table upon an earthen floor, I fell into conversation with Judge Ames, the talented, good-hearted but eccentric editor of the San Diego *Herald*, of whom the poet Andrews in his immortal work *The Cocopa Maid* once profanely sang as follows:

> *There was a man whose name was Ames,*
> *His aims were aims of mystery;*
> *His story odd, I think by —*
> *Would make a famous history.*

I found "the Judge" exceedingly agreeable, urbane and well-informed, and obtained from him much valuable information regarding San Diego and its statistics.

San Diego contains at present about seven hundred inhabitants, two-thirds of whom are "native and to the manor born." The remainder is a mixture of American, English, German, Hebrew and Pike County. There are seven stores or shops in the village, where anything might be obtained from a fine-toothed comb to a horse rake, two public houses, a Catholic church which meets in a private residence, and a Protestant *ditto,* to which the Rev. Dr. Reynolds, chaplain of the miliatry post six miles distant, communicates religious intelligence every Sunday afternoon.

San Diego is the residence of Don Juan Bandini whose mansion fronts one side of the Plaza. He is well known to the early settlers of California as a gentleman of distinguished politeness and hospitality. His wife and daughters are among the most beautiful and accomplished ladies of our State. One of the latter is married to Mr. Sterns, a very wealthy and distinguished resident of Los Angelos, another to Col. Couts, late a lieutenant in the first regiment of U.S. dragoons, and another to Mr. Charles Johnson, who for a long time was the agent of the P.M.S.S. Company at this place. The whole family is highly connected and universally respected.

Having smoked the pipe of contemplation and played a game of billiards with a young gentleman who remarked "he could give me fifty and beat me," which he certainly did with a celerity that led me to conclude "he couldn't do anything else," I retired for the night, but not to sleep, as I fondly imagined.

Fleas? Rather! I say nothing at present; my feelings of indignation against those wretched insects are too deep for utterance. On another occasion, when in a milder mood, I intend to write a letter concerning and condemnatory of them, and publish it. Yes, by Heaven, if I have to pay for it as an advertisement!

The next morning, bright and early, I parted with my young military friend McAuburn who was about to join his company at the Gila River.

"Goodbye, Phoenix," says he, "God bless you, old fellow! And look here, if you go to San Francisco, tell her — no, by George! You always make fun of everything. Goodbye."

So he wrung my hand and galloped away, and I stood looking after him till his prancing horse and graceful figure were hid by the projecting hills of the old Presidio.

"Blessings go with you, my boy!" said I, "for a fine, honest, noble-hearted young chap you haven't many superiors in the U.S. Army. And happy, in my opinion, is the woman who gets you."

How I went to a *Baile* and visited New Town, and rode forth to the Mission, and attended a *Fiesta*, and the extraordinary adventures that befell me there, shall form the subject of a future epistle; at present my time is too much occupied, for lo, *I am an editor!* Hasn't Ames gone to San Francisco (with this very letter in his pocket) leaving a notice in his last edition "that during his absence an able literary friend will assume his position as editor of the *Herald*," and am I not that able literary friend? (Heaven save the mark).

"You'd better believe it."

I've been writing a "leader" and funny anecdotes all day (which will account for the dryness of this production) and *such* a "leader" and *such* anecdotes.

I'll send you a paper next week, and if you don't allow that there's been no such publication, weekly or serial since the days of the "Bunkum Flagstaff," I'll *craw fish* and take to reading Johnson's Dictionary. Fraternally — ahem!

Yours.

97

SAN DIEGO HERALD.

Independent in all Things — Neutral in Nothing!!

The first newspaper in San Diego was a four-page, news-mongering sheet called the San Diego *Herald,* edited and published by Judson Ames. Although he arrived penniless in San Francisco on October, 1849, Ames — who was sometimes called "The Judge" or "Boston" — made friends quickly, and by December he was entrenched in the political and social network of El Dorado. One of his influential friends was Governor John Bigler, who ran the Democratic party political machine. Another influential acquaintance was Senator William H. Gwin, a transplanted Tennessean, who hoped to extend southern influence into California by bringing settlers from the South into California via the transcontinental railroad.

Jud Ames fit into these grandiose plans as the publisher of the San Diego *Herald.* In December, 1850 Ames arrived in San Diego and passed out prospectus and advertising contracts for his new newspaper. He succeeded in transporting a Washington Press across the Isthmus of Panama, and set up shop initially in "New Town" San Diego, where the first edition appeared on May 29, 1851. When the "New Town" settlement failed temporarily, Ames moved his press to the northwest corner of the plaza in Old Town.

News items were so scarce in the sleepy little village of San Diego (population 700) that Ames would sometimes publish the names of unclaimed letters at the post office. But for the most part, early editions of the newspaper were filled with the activities of the Atlantic-Pacific Railroad Committee and with the detailed reports of the local Democratic Party Caucus, of which Ames was secretary. To further help his political patrons, in July, 1853, Ames dedicated a large portion of his newspaper to advocating the Democratic ticket in the forthcoming Gubernatorial election.

As a reward for his political allegiance, the San Francisco political bosses filled Judson Ames's tiny newspaper with advertisements. In addition, Governor Bigler pushed a bill through the legislature that required all legal notices in San Diego and San Bernardino Counties to be published in the *Herald*. Ames happily announced on July 9, 1853 that "His Excellency, Governor Bigler" had also appointed him Notary Public under the new law, and the editor of the *Herald* informed advertisers that he had purchased new lead type and engravings in anticipation of their advertising needs.

S. DIEGO ADVERTISEMENTS.

J. Judson Ames,

NOTARY PUBLIC,

UNDER THE NEW LAW.

CONVEYANCER and
GENERAL AGENT.
COMMISSIONER IN CALIFORNIA
to take Acknowledgments, Depositions, Affidavits, etc., for the States of *Mississippi* and *Louisiana*.

Agreements, Deeds, Mortgages, Certificates of Incorporation, Powers of Attorney, Charter Parties, Bottomry Bonds. Bills of Sale of Vessels and other Commercial Papers drawn and acknowledged. Protests of vessels noted and extended.

Most of the Judson Ames's time was spent traveling to and from San Francisco, securing advertising and meeting with politicians. It was on such a trip to San Francisco in August, 1853, that he selected Lt. George Derby as an interim editor. The *Herald* of August 20, 1853 contained the following announcement:

> *"Next week, with Divine Assistance, a new hand will be applied to the bellows of this establishment, and an intensely interesting issue will possibly be the result. The paper will be published on Wednesday evening; and, to avoid confusion, the crowd will please form in the plaza passing four abreast by the city hall and Herald office, from the gallery of which Johnny will hand them their papers. "E pluribus unum," or a word to the wise is bastante."*

Derby, still cooling his heels on the San Diego River diversion project, was a likely choice for interim editor. Derby and Ames had perhaps met at a meeting of the Masons, of which they were both active members, and Derby, *alias* John Phoenix, had become one of the literary wits of the frontier.

As a fellow Mason, Ames trusted Derby implicitly, but he forgot to give the prankster detailed instructions on how he wanted the *Herald* run during his absence. Under Ames, the *Herald* strongly supported the re-election of John Bigler, who was the Democratic candidate for re-election as governor. But Derby was a Whig, then known as the Reform Party, and Governor Bigler was also one of Squibob's favorite poltical targets. Never one to allow a joke to pass, upon Judge Ames's departure for San Francisco, the lieutenant quickly changed into his literary disguise and became "John Phoenix, the mad wag." On August 24, 1853, the new editor of the San Diego *Herald* promptly reversed the paper's politcal line and urged voters to vote for the "Phoenix Independent Ticket," headed by William Waldo for Governor.

THE PHOENIX TICKET

*First printed in the San Diego
Herald, August 24, 1853*

SAN DIEGO, August 24, 1853. *"FACILIS descensus Averni,"* which may be liberally, not literally translated; It is easy to go to San Francisco. Big Ames has gone; departed in the *Goliah*, in the hope of obtaining new advertisements for this interesting journal, perchance hoping also to be paid for the old ones. I hope he may succeed in both endeavors. During his absence, which I trust will not exceed two weeks, I am to remain in charge of the *Herald*, the literary part thereof — I would beg to be understood — the *responsible* portion of the editorial duties falling upon my friend Johnny who had, in the kindest manner, undertaken "the fighting department," and to whom I hereby refer any pugnacious or bellicose individual who may take offense at the tone of any of my leaders. The public at large, therefore, will understand that I stand upon "Josh Haven's platform," which

For the People.

The voters of San Diego county are requested to examine carefully the following ticket, to make such alterations therein as they may deem proper, and then, to cut it from the paper, and deposit it in some secure place, in readiness for the day of election.

PHŒNIX INDEPENDENT TICKET.

For Governor,
WILLIAM WALDO.

For Lieutenant Governor,
SAMUEL PURDY.

For Treasurer of State,
RICHARD ROMAN.

For Comptroller,
SAM. BELL, of Mariposa.

For Justice of the Supreme Court,
TOD ROBINSON, of Sacramento.

For Attorney General,
J. R. McCONNELL, of Nevada.

For Surveyor General
SELIM E. WOODWORTH, of Mt'y

For Superintendent of Public Instruc.
SHERMAN DAY, of Santa Clara.

For Senator,
J. P. McFARLAND.

For Member of Assembly,
W. C. FERRELL.

For County Judge.
JOHN HAYES.

For Clerk County Court.
PHILLIP CROSTHWAITE,

For Sheriff
FRANCIS HINTON.

For District Attorney
J. W. ROBINSON.

For Treasurer.
LEWIS ROSE.

For County Surveyor.
CHARLES H. POOLE.

For Public Administrator
W. H. MOON.

For Coroner.
L. STRAUSS.

For Assessor.
GEO. LYONS.

For Justices of the Peace.
P. H. HOOFF.   D. H. ROGERS.

For Constables.
C. MORRIS.   R. ISRAEL

that gentleman defined some years since to be the liberty of saying anything he pleased about anybody, without considering himself at all responsible. It is an exceedingly free and independent position, and rather agreeable than otherwise; but I have no disposition whatever to abuse it.

It will be perceived that I have not availed myself of the editorial privilege of using the plural pronoun in referring to myself. This is simply because I consider it a ridiculous affectation. I am a "lone, lorn man," unmarried (the Lord be praised for his infinite mercy), and though blessed with a consuming appetite "which causes the keepers of the house where I board (Hooff & Ebbetts) to tremble." I do not think I have a tape worm, therefore I have no claim whatever to call myself "we," and shall by no means fall into that editorial absurdity.

San Diego has been usually dull during the past week, and a summary of the news may be summarily disposed of. There have been no births, no marriages, no arrivals, no departures, no earthquakes, nothing but the usual number of drinks taken and an occasional "small chunk of a fight" (in which no lives have been lost) to vary the monotony of our existence. Placidly sat our village worthies in the arm-chairs in front of the "Exchange," puffing their short clay pipes and enjoying their "*otium cum dignitate.*" a week ago, and placidly they sit there still.

The changes in the moon have occurred with their usual regularity, "Fine as silk, but not, half so well beliked by the ladies," one day, and "very poorly, thank God, how are you yourself, I thank you, sir," the next.

I said there had been no arrivals: I referred to individuals, not steamers, for the *Stephens* touched here from Panama in the early part of the week, and the *Goliah* from San Francisco a day or two after, but they went away again, and nothing came of it. The only topic of interest now discussed among us is the approaching election, and on this subject I desire to say a few words:

Let the voters of this country remember that on the selection of their legislative officers depends their peace, prosperity and well-being, and it may be the life and liberty of some among them during the ensuing year. With this serious reflection, let them consider well before depositing a vote for a man to fill a responsible station, and then act upon their convictions uninfluenced by gratuitious drinks of wretched whiskey, or the fact that he is called by one party of another.

Party lines, my brother voters of San Diego, have become obliterated. Since the last general election the only distinction between the great Democratic party of the United States and their opponents is in the name. Difference of principle no longer exists. The National Bank has long since been levelled low; the great Tariff question has been finally put at rest, and the important Whig policy of Internal Improvements has become a plank of the Democratic platform.

To those old soldiers who were with us before the adoption of the Constitution and, in consequence, are entitled to vote, I would say: remember, my lads, that the duty of a good soldier in time of peace is to be an estimable citizen and, as such, to assist in the election of good men to office. The man who seeks your vote for any office by furnishing you with whiskey, gratis, and credit at his little shop (if he happens to keep one, is by no means calculated to be either a good maker or dispenser of the laws. Drink his whiskey, by all means, if you like it and he invites you, but make him no pledges and on the day of election vote any other ticket than that he gives you. You know well enough, oh! My soldiers, how much he cares for you, and can appreciate his professions of attachment. They amount to precisely the same as those of Jacob, who bought the birthright of Esau for a mess of pottage. Don't barter yours for a little whiskey, and make for the country a worse mess than Esau could ever have concocted.

Should any gentleman, differing with me in opinion feel anxious "to give utterance to the thought," I can only say, my dear sir, the *Herald* is a neutral paper and while I have charge of it, its light shall shine for all; express yourself, therefore, fully, but concisely, in an ably written article; hand it to me and I will, with pleasure, present it to the world through the columns of this wide-spread journal, merely reserving for myself the privilege of using you up, as I shall infallibly do, and to a fearful extent, if facts are facts, reason is reasonable and "I know myself intimately," of which, at present, I have no manner of doubt.

And thus having said my say in a plain, straightforward manner, which I think will exonerate the *Herald* this week from the charge of being of uncertain aims, I shall close for the present with the assurance to the public that I remain their obedient, and particularly humble servant,

John Phoenix

Frank, our accomplished compositor, who belongs to the fighting wing of the unterrified Democracy "groans in spirit, and is troubled," as he sets up our heretical doctrines and opinions. He says "the Whigs will be delighted with the paper this week."

We hope so. We know several respectable gentlemen who are Whigs, and feel anxious to delight them, as well as our Democratic friends (of whose approval we are confident) and all other sorts and conditions of men, always excepting Biglerites and Abolitionists.

"Ah" sighs the unfortunate Frank, "but what *will* Ames say when he gets back?"

Haven't the slightest idea; we shall probably ascertain by reading the first Herald published after his return. Meanwhile, we devoutly hope that event will not take place before we've had a chance to give Mr. Bigler one *blizzard* on the subjects of "Water-front extension," and "State printing." We understand these schemes fully and are inclined to enlighten the public of San Diego with regard to them.

Ah, Bigler, my boy, "old is J.B. but cunning, sir and *devilish sly*." Phoenix is after you, and you'd better pray for the return of the editor *de facto* to San Diego, while yet there is time, or you're a *goner*, as far as this county is concerned.

PHOENIX AS EDITOR

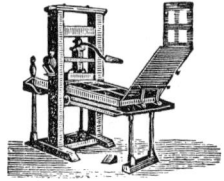

"THERE'S MANY A SLIP 'TWEEN THE CUP AND THE LIP." *Proverbs 53, 14.*

San Diego Herald, September 3, 1853

It was my intention to have devoted about two columns of this journal, this week, to an exposition of the nefarious scheme of the "Water Front Extension," at San Francisco, and the abuse of the gubernatorial power that has been exercised in the matter of the "State Printing," during the past year.

But I have been deterred from doing all this by two good and sufficient reasons. In the first place, I can find but one man in the county who ever intended to vote for Bigler, and I have labored with him to prove the errors of opinion into which he has fallen, to that extent, that partly from the effects of the Fiesta at San Luis Rey (where, as a matter of course, he became excessively inebriated) and, partly from agitation of mind produced by my arguments, he has fallen into a violent fit of sickness from which his physician thinks he cannot possibly recover before the day of election. And, secondly, I have a horrible misgiving that the editor *de facto* will return before this edition has gone to press, in which case, coming down on me from San Francisco "like a young giant refreshed with new wine," and finding (what he would consider) such abominable heresy in his columns, he would doubtless knock the whole matter into *pi*, and perhaps, in the extremity of his wrath, inflict some grievous bodily injury on me, all of which would be intensely disagreeable. Moved by these considerations, therefore, I shall let John Bigler entirely alone, and in the case of his re-election, shall make a great merit of having done so, and apply to him immediately for a commission as Notary Public.

The great event of the past week has been the Fiesta at San Luis Rey. Many of our citizens attended, and a very large number of native Californians and Indians collected from the various ranchos in the vicinity. High mass was celebrated in the old church on Thursday morning, an Indian baby was baptised, another nearly killed by being run over by an excited individual on an excited horse, and that day and the following were passed in witnessing the absurd efforts of some twenty natives to annoy a number of tame bulls with the tips of their horns cut off. This great national amusement, ironically termed bull-fighting, consists in waving a *serape*, or handkerchief, in front of the bull until he is sufficiently annoyed to run after his tormentor, when that individual gets out of his way, with great precipitation. The nights were passed in an equally intellectual manner.

The "Phoenix Ticket" *generally,* appears to give general satisfaction. It was merely put forward suggestively, and not being the result of a clique of convention, the public are at liberty to make such alterations or erasures as they may think proper. I hope it may meet with a strong support on the day of the election; but should it meet with defeat, I shall endeavor to bear the inevitable mortification that must result, with my usual equanimity.

Like unto the great Napoleon after the battle of Waterloo, or the magnanimous Boggs after his defeat in the gubernatorial campaign of Missouri, I shall fold my arms with tranquility and say either *"C'est fini,"* or *"Oh shaw, I know'd it."*

Though this is but my second bow to a San Diego audience, I presume it to be my last appearance and valedictory for the editor will doubtless arrive before another week elapses — the gun will be removed from my trembling grasp, and the *Herald* will resume its great aims and heavy firing, and I hope will discharge its debt to the public with accuracy and precision. Meanwhile "The Lord be with you."

"BE VIRTUOUS AND YOU WILL BE HAPPY."

We have received for publication an article signed "LEONIDAS," from the pen of an old and esteemed friend of ours, intended to counteract the effect of our leader last week, which we should publish were it not for its length and the rather strong style in which it is written. Many of the principle points of Leonidas' opposition are removed in this issue of the paper, and we doubt if it would serve any useful purpose to publish extracts from his letter, or if he would be pleased with our doing so.

He winds up exhorting the Democrats "to keep together" (we hope they will, it would give us unfeigned regret to see any man explode or fall to pieces), and by calling us, indirectly, "*a rabid Whig.*"

In this, Leonidas, you are mistaken. Our ideas on political matters are precisely those of the lamented Joseph Bowers, who when running for the office of —— in the state of —— was asked by the —— committee, "Mr. Bowers, what are your politics?"

To which he replied, "Gentlemen, I have no politics."

"What," exclaimed the committee in surprise, "no politics?"

"No, gentlemen," rejoined the imperturbable Joseph, "not a d—d politic."

He was elected unanimously, as many of our readers from — will doubtless remember, and we hope, should it ever come to pass that we are a candidate for public office, we may meet with the like good fortune.

So farewell, oh Leonidas, we trust you are not yet "boiling with indignation;" but if unhappily that is the case, we can only placidly remark — "*Boil on.*"

WANTED — By the subscriber, a serious young man, with fixed principles of integrity and sobriety, to make beds, sweep a room, black boots and bring water. For a youth of religious principles, to whom a large salary is not of so much object as a knowledge of the business, an eligible situation is here offered.

We carelessly threw a bucket of water from our office door the other day, the most of which fell upon an astonished Spaniard, sitting upon his horse before the Colorado House. He made the brief remark "*Carajo,*" meaning that we were courageous, and on observing his stalwart form, and the ferocity of his expression and moustaches, we thought we were.

FOR SALE — A valuable Law Library, lately the property of a distinguished legal gentleman of San Francisco, who has given up the practice and removed to the Farralone Islands. It consists of one volume of Hoyles' Games, complete, and may be seen at this office.

ELECTION RESULTS

After the *Herald's* political somersault, the unthinkable happened: William Waldo, the Whig candidate for governor, actually carried San Diego County! Of course, outside of San Diego where the Democratic machine was still in control, Bigler easily won the necessary votes for victory. As the election results of September 7th were tabulated, Derby noted with chagrin that the entire Mormon population of one district had voted for Bigler. Derby added sarcastically that one might as well have polled the residents of Yerba Buena Island on the San Francisco Bay — where the only inhabitants were goats! Derby was even happier to receive a letter from a doctor at the State Lunatic Asylum in Stockton requesting copies of the *Herald* for his patients' reading room.

"Now this is encouraging," Derby wrote. "After laboring two weeks with unremitting ardor to establish for this paper a literary character secondary to none in the Union, we at last have our exertions rewarded, by the addition to our subscription list of a whole Lunatic Asylum!"

Most of the citizens of Old San Diego were delighted with the 180 degree shift in politics and convulsed with laughter at the way a second lieutenant had "bamboozled" Judson Ames, the publisher of the San Diego *Herald*. Copies of the newspaper were picked up by passing steamers, and the *Herald* was widely reprinted by Eastern newspapers, who described Derby's prank as one of the great jokes of the wild, and unpredictable frontier.

Although some historians believe that Judson Ames was in on the joke and the entire episode was a well-laid plot, in the the following article the prankster editor imagines the scene in which Ames first learns of the switch in the newspaper's political endorsement.

DEMOCRATIC STATE NOMINATIONS,

Subject to the Decision of the State Democratic Convention, May, 1855.

FOR GOVERNOR,

JOHN BIGLER.

FOR LIEUT. GOVERNOR,

SAMUEL PURDY.

San Diego Herald, September 24, 1853

☞ **THE COMEDY OF ERRORS** — We have been accused, with great injustice, of a "reckless propensity to lampoon." We disclaim, with indignation, any such propensity. On the contrary, such has been our anxiety to avoid personalities, or unpleasant allusions, that we have actually suppressed some of the very funniest things we have ever heard — little drolleries over which we have laughed, ourselves, in the sanctity of the sanctum, until the "armchair" has cracked again, and wondering men in the billiard room below have poked up against the ceiling with their cues (that they might take their cue from us) simply because the mention of some name, Jones, Brown or Muggins, has rendered us unable to present them to the public. The conductor of a public journal is responsible for everything that he presents, and he should never indulge in personalities, however humorous they may appear, or however much they may amuse himself, or be calculated to amuse his readers.

It is for this reason that we forbear publishing the following capital thing, dramatized expressly for our paper, and which we are solemnly assured, occurred very nearly, if not exactly, as represented.

SCENE. — The interior of the City Post Office at San Francisco, Governor B— discovered, sitting, holding a copy of the San Francisco *Herald* at arms' length, in a pair of tongs, and reading it with every mark of scorn and deep disgust. Enter Judge A. from the South, Editor of the San Diego *Herald*.

Judge A. Ah! Governor, your most obedient; how do you do, sir?

Governor B. (Putting the *Herald* in a bucket of water, and laying down the tongs. How do you do, A., how d'ye do? Well, how are matters going on in San Diego County?

Judge A. Oh! Admirably; you may depend on the unanimous support of that county, sir, the *Herald* has an immense, a commanding influence there, it will be felt, sir. I have left the paper in the charge of an able literary friend there, sir, Mr. Phoenix; probably you may have heard of him, a man of great ability; I expect an admirable paper from him this week, sir.

Governor B. (With a bland smile). Ah! Thorough Democrat, eh?

Judge A. Oh! Certainly; I never thought to ask him, but — oh, of course, certainly he is a Democrat.

Governor B. Oh! Certainly; I shall be glad to see his paper, Mr. A., ah! Very glad, sir.

Here the mail is opened, the judge eagerly receives a bundle of the first Phoenix *Herald*, hastily tears off the envelope, hands one copy to the Governor, and takes another himself. Each put on spectacles and glance at the first column, where appears in fatal capitals the respectable name of William Waldo. Grand Tableau!!! The Governor and the Judge gaze at each other over the tops of their respective papers, the one with wrathful and indignant glance, the other with the most concentrated expression of horror and misery of which the human countenance is capable.

(Here the Ghost of old Squibob himself (ought to have been) seen rising, and hovering for an instant over the pair in an attitude of benediction, murmuring, "Bless ye, my children," larfs and disappears in a "sweet scented" cloud.)

We forbear to give the conversation that ensued — this is a Christian community in which we live and the introduction of excessive profanity in the columns of a public journal, even as a quotation, would not and ought not to be tolerated.

We have received by the *Goliah* an affecting letter from Judge Ames, beseeching us to return to the fold of Democracy, from which he is inclined to intimate we have been straying. Is it possible that we have been laboring under a delusion — and that Waldo is a Whig! Why! lor! How singular! But anxious to atone for our past errors, willing to please the taste of the Editor, and above all, ever solicitous to be on the strong side, we gladly abjure our former opinions, embrace Democracy with ardor, slap her on the back, declare ourselves in favor of erecting a statue of Andrew Jackson in the Plaza, and to prove our sincerity, run up to-day at the end of our columns, a Democratic ticket for 1855, which we hope will please the most fastidious. Being rather hard up for principles for our political faith, we have commenced the study of the back numbers of the Democratic Review, and finding therein that **"DEMOCRACY IS THE SUPREMACY OF MAN OVER HIS ACCIDENTS,"** we hereby express our contempt for a man with a sprained ankle, and unmitigated scorn for anybody who may be kicked by a mule or a woman. That's Democratic, ain't it? Oh, we understand these things. Bless your soul, Judge, we're a Democrat.

Judson Ames was gone for six weeks, not two weeks as originally planned, and as each day passed the interim editor cautiously eyed the passing steamers in anticipation of the editor's return. There was reason for Derby to fear "the Judge." Ames was a huge figure of a man — six foot six and a half inches tall — and had once killed a man during a fight in the Boston harbor. In the October 1, 1853 issue, which was Derby's last as "guest" editor, John Phoenix humorously imagines the confrontation between himself and a furious Judson Ames.

RETURN OF THE EDITOR

First Printed in the San Diego Herald, October 1, 1853

SAN DIEGO, SATURDAY **October 1, 1853.** *"Te Deum Laudamus."* Judge Ames has returned! With the completion of this article my labors are ended; and wiping my pen on my coat-tail and placing it behind my sinister ear with graceful bow and bland smile for my honored admirers, and a wink of intense meaning for my enemies, I shall abdicate, with dignity, the "Arm-chair," in favor of its legitimate proprietor.

By the way, this "Arm-Chair" is but a pleasant fiction of Boston's — the only seat in the *Herald* office being the empty nail keg, which I have occupied while writing my leaders upon the inverted sugar box that answers the purpose of a table. But such is life. Divested of its poetry and romance, the objects of our highest admiration become common-places, like the *Herald's* chair and table. Many ideas which we have learned to love and reverence, from the poetry of imagination, as tables, become old sugar boxes on close inspection and more intimate acquaintance.

"Sic —" but I forbear that sickening and hackneyed quotation.

During the period in which I have had control over the *Herald* I have endeavored to the best of my ability to amuse and interest its readers, and I cannot but hope that my good humored efforts have proved successful. If I have given offense to any by the tone of my remarks, I assure them that it has been quite unintentional, and to prove that I bear no malice I hereby accept their apologies. Certainly no one can complain of a lack of versatility in the last six numbers. Commencing as an Independent Journal, I have gradually passed through all the stages of incipient Whiggery, decided Conservatism, dignified Recantation, budding Democracy, and rampant Radicalism, and I now close the series with an entirely literary number, in which I have carefully abstained from the mention of Baldo and Wigler, I mean Wagler and Bildo, no — never mind — as Toodles says, I haven't mentioned any of 'em, but been careful to preserve a perfect armed neutrality.

The paper this week will be found particularly stupid. This is the result of deep design on my part; had I attempted anything remarkably brilliant, you would all have detected it and said, probably with truth; "Ah, this is Phoenix's last appearance, he has tried to be very funny and has made a miserable failure of it. Hee! Hee! Hee!"

Oh! no, my public, an ancient weasel may not be detected in the act of slumber in that manner. I was well aware of all this, and have been as dull and prosy as possible to avoid it. Very little news will be found in the *Herald* this week: the fact is, there never is much news in it, and it is very well that it is so; the climate here is so delightful that residents, in the enjoyment of the *dolce far niente*, care very little about what is going on elsewhere, and residents in other places care very little about what is going on in San Diego, so all parties are likely to be gratified with the little paper, "and long may it wave."

In conclusion, I am gratified to be able to state that Johnny's office (the fighting department), for the last six weeks, has been a sinecure, and with the exception of the atrocious conduct of one miscreant, who was detected very early one morning in the act of chalking **"ASS"** on our office door, and who was dismissed with a harmless kick and a gentle admonition that he should not write his name on other persons' property, our course has been peaceful, and undisturbed by any expression of an unpleasant nature.

So, farewell Public, I hope you will do well; I do, upon my soul. This leader is ended, and if there be any man among you who thinks he could write a better one, let him try it, and if he succeeds I shall merely remark that I could have done it myself if I had tried. Adios!

Respectfully Yours,
John Phoenix

Ye That Suffer,
Read! Read!!· Read!!!

DR. PAREIRAS'
Great Italian Remedy!

"INTERVIEW" BETWEEN BOSTON AND PHOENIX

San Diego Herald, October 1, 1853

The *Thomas Hunt* had arrived, she lay at the wharf at New Town, and a rumor had reached our ears that "The Judge" was on board. Public anxiety had been excited to the highest pitch to witness the result of the meeting between us. It had been stated publicly that the "Judge" would whip us the moment he arrived; but though we thought a conflict probable, we had never been very successful as to its terminating in this manner. Cooly we gazed from the window of the Office upon the New Town road; we descried a cloud of dust in the distance; high above it waved a whip lash, and we said, "The Judge" cometh, and his driving is like that of Jehu, the son of Nimshi, for he driveth furiously."

Calmly we seated ourselves in the "arm-chair," and continued our labors upon our magnificent Pictorial. Anon a step, a heavy step, was heard upon the stairs and the Judge stood before us.

"In shape and gesture proudly eminent, stood like a tower: ... but his face deep scars of thunder had entrenched, and care sat on his faded cheek; but under brows of dauntless courage and considerate pride, waiting revenge."

We rose, and with an unfaltering voice said:
"Well, Judge, how do you do?"
He made no reply, but commences taking off his coat.
We removed ours, also our cravat.

The sixth and last round is described by the pressman and compositors as having been fearing scientific. We held the Judge down over the press by our nose (which we had inserted between his teeth for that purpose), and while our hair was employed in holding one of his hands, we held the other in our left, and with the "sheep's foot" brandished above our head, shouted to him, "Say Waldo."

"Never!" he gasped —

Oh! My Bigler he would have muttered,
But that he "dried us," ere the word was uttered.

At this moment, we discovered that we had been laboring under a "misunderstanding," and through the amicable intervention of the pressman, who thrust a roller between our faces (which gave the whole affair a very different complexion, the matter was finally settled on the most friendly terms — "and without prejudice to the honor of either party."

We write this while sitting without clothing, except our left stocking, and the rim of our hat encircling our neck like a "ruff" of the Elizabethan era — that article of dress having been knocked over our head at an early stage of the proceedings, and the crown subsequently torn off — while the Judge is sopping his eye with cold water in the next room, a small boy standing beside the sufferer with a basin, and glancing with interest over the advertisements on the second page of the San Diego *Herald*, a fair copy of which was struck off upon the back of his shirt at the time we held him over the press. Thus ends our description of this long-anticipated personal collision, of which the public can believe precisely as much as they please; if they disbelieve the whole of it, we shall not be at all offended, but can simply quote as much to the point, what might have been the commencement of our epitaph, had we fallen in the conflict,

"HERE LIES PHOENIX"

"PHOENIX'S PICTORIAL"

As John Phoenix bid his readers farewell, the prankster Derby couldn't resist one final opportunity to burlesque the increasingly popular trend among newspapers of the time to illustrate their stories with "special engravings."

PHŒNIX'S PICTORIAL,

And Second Story Front Room Companion.

Vol. I.]	San Diego, October 1, 1853.	[No. I.

Portrait of His Royal Highness Prince Albert.—Prince Albert, the son of a gentleman named Coburg, is the husband of Queen Victoria of England, and the father of many of her children. He is the inventor of the celebrated "Albert hat," which has been lately introduced with great effect in the U. S. Army. The Prince is of German extraction, his father being a Dutchman and his mother a Duchess.

Mansion of John Phœnix, Esq., San Diego, California.

House in which Shakespeare was born, in Stratford-on-Avon.

Abbotsford, the residence of Sir Walter Scott, author of Byron's Pilgrim's Progress, &c.

The Capitol at Washington.

Residence of Governor Bigler, at Benicia, California.

Battle of Lake Erie, (*see remarks*, p. 96.)

[Page 96.]

The Battle of Lake Erie, of which our Artist presents spirited engraving, copied from the original painting, by Hannibal Carracci, in the possession of J. P. Haven, Esq., was fought in 1836, on Chesapeake Bay, between the U. S. Frigates Constitution and Guerriere and the British Troops under General Putnam. Our glorious flag, there as everywhere was victorious, and " Long may it wave, o'er the land of the free, and the home of *the slave.*"

Fearful accident on the Camden & Amboy Railroad ! !
Terrible loss of life ! ! !

View of the City of San Diego, by Sir Benjamin West.

Interview between Mrs. Harriet Beecher Stowe and the
Duchess of Sutherland, from a group of Statuary, by Clarke
Mills.

Bank Account of J. Phœnix, Esq., at Adams & Co.
Bankers, San Francisco, California

Gas Works, San Diego Herald Office.

Steamer Goliah.

View of a California Ranch.—Landseer.

Shell of an Oyster once eaten by General Washington, showing the General's manner of opening Oysters.

There !—this is but a specimen of what we can do if liberally sustained. We wait with anxiety to hear the verdict of the Public, before proceeding to any farther and greater outlays.

Subscription, $5 per annum, payable invariably in advance.

INDUCEMENTS FOR CLUBBING.

Twenty Copies furnished for one year, for fifty cents. Address John Phœnix, Office of the San Diego Herald.

SECOND EDITION!

Such has been the demand for the back numbers of the "Phœnix" Herald, that our editions have been entirely exhausted, and we have at last concluded to have the whole of them stereotyped. We have now seven hundred and eighty-two Indians employed night and day in mixing adobe for the type moulds, and as no suitable metal is to be found in San Diego, to cast the stereotypes, we have engaged 324,000 ball cartridges, from the Mission, for the sake of the lead. A very serious accident came near occurring in our office this morning, owing to the ignition of a cartridge, caused by friction, resulting from the rapid manner in which it was unrolled, but fortunately we escaped, with slight loss, one of our compositors having had his leg fractured just above the knee joint. The injured member was promptly and neatly taken off by "Phœnix," with a broad-axe in 2.46, and the sufferer is now doing well and engaged in setting type with his teeth. Our steam roller presses having failed to arrive (owing to the non arrival of the Goliah, as a matter of course), we have been obliged to work off the Pictorial Herald on our solitary Power Press.

"The Press is a tremendous engine." We have two tremendous Indians working at ours. Four men remove the papers as fast as printed, and forming a line to the outer door, four boys distribute them from the gallery to the excited crowd below.

Nothing is heard but the monotonous *houp! hank!* of the Indians, as in a cloud of steam of their own manufacture they strike off the paper. Nothing can be seen without but a shower of quarters, bits, and dimes darkening the air as they are thrown from the purchasers. Fourteen bushels and three pecks of silver have been received since we commenced distribution, and the cry is still they come.

THIRD EDITION!!

Fatal Accident!

A MELANCHOLY accident has just taken place. A fleshy gentleman had received a copy of the "Pictorial," and retired to the foot of the Flag-staff to peruse it. He had glanced over the first column, when he was observed to grow black in the face. A bystander hastened to seize him by the collar, but it was too late! Exploding with mirth, he was scattered into a thousand fragments, one of which striking him, probably inflicted some fatal injury, as he immediately expired, having barely time to remove his hat, and say in a feeble voice, "Give this to Phœnix." A large back tooth lies on the table before us, driven through the side of the office with fearful violence at the time of the explosion. We have enclosed it to his widow with a letter of condolence. The name of the unfortunate man was MUGGINS!

FOURTH EDITION!!!

The Very Latest!!!

MRS. MUGGINS has just been picking up the fragments of the deceased in a hand-basket. We omitted to state that the tooth had been filled by Dr. R. E. Cole, Dentist, whose advertisement may be found in another column! In her frantic agony the bereaved widow has accused us of purloining the gold. A terrible scene has ensued in our office, in consequence—after much recrimination between us, we have been atrociously "clapper-clawed" by Mrs. Muggins!

125

A LITTLE MORE FOR THE VERY LAST!!

After great exertion the fragments have been put together by Dr. H——, and the Muggins family have retired to their home, each bearing a copy of the "Pictorial," in triumph before them. Old Muggins has presented us with the tooth, and it may be seen at our office.

PHOENIX OUTFOXED

"Phoenix has played the 'Devil' during our absence," Ames wrote in the San Diego *Herald* upon his return, "but he has done it in such good humored manner that we have not a word to say ... Well, it is over, Bigler is Governor and the country is safe for the next two years, at least."

The confrontation Derby feared with Judson Ames never materialized, and Derby now turned his attention to the San Diego River Project, which needed to be completed before the winter rains set in. To his disappointment, the Board of Engineers had chosen the least expensive of his proposals — namely to excavate sand from the old river bed and build a protecting levee from Old Town to an opposite point on Playa Road. Although Derby raised personal reservations about the success of this trimmed down version, he set about energetically to accomplish the task, and by November, 1853 the primary work had been completed. But the funds were insufficient to finish the protecting levee, and the lieutenant was forced to await another appropriation by Congress.

As the winter storms approached, Derby's personal life was also in turmoil. He couldn't get over Mary Coons, but was too stubborn to break his oath and return to San Francisco. Thus, legend has it, Mary Angelina Coons was forced to snag Derby as a husband through a clever ploy. Mary's mother had decided to return to St. Louis, and although the daughter had no intention of leaving San Francisco, Mary placed an item in the local newspaper announcing her departure from San Francisco by winter steamer. When Derby read the news he was panic-stricken and caught the next steamer to San Francisco. In January, 1854, the following item appeared:

⤝⤞⤟ *MARRIED* ⤠⤡⤢

In Trinity Church, San Francisco, January 14th, by the Rev. Dr. Clark, Lieut. George H. Derby, U.S. Corps of Topographical Engineers, to Mary A. Coons of St. Louis, Mo.

Immediately after the ceremony, the bridal party repaired on board the steamer, Southerner, after partaking of a magnificent déjeuner à la fourchette, given in honor of the occurence by J. Nugent, Esq., and other friends, and sailed at 4 p.m. for San Diego.

The newly-weds moved into a two-story home on Harney Street that had been prefabricated in Massachusetts and shipped around the Horn to San Diego. Derby would often sit in the upstairs bedroom of the cottage and write his sketches for the *Herald* or detail the progress of the San Diego River Project in his letters to Colonel Abert. Currently known as the Derby-Pendleton house, in 1962 the house was moved out of the path of a freeway to its present location in Old Town, where San Diego visitors can view Derby relics, including one of the topographical engineer's dress uniforms. Across the street is "Squibob Square," named in honor of Lt. George Derby's contributions to early San Diego.

Map of Lieut Derby.

Note, The figure marked A is an elevation of Mrs D.

1854

Courtesy The Bancroft Library

The San Diego River project became wearisome, and Derby spent months in the dreary village of San Diego awaiting appropriations from Congress to complete the project. He was sent out from Washington, Derby noted gloomily, "to dam the San Diego River," and ended up "damning San Diego."

The scaled down version of the levee, which eventually extended from Old Town to Playa Road, also gave the lieutenant the ironic distinction of building a dam almost *parallel* to the San Diego River, not *across* it.

4th of JULY CELEBRATION

Reported Expressly for the San Diego Herald (1854)

TUESDAY LAST, the 4th of July being the anniversary of the discovery of San Diego by the Hon. J.J. Warner in 1846, as well as that of our National Independence ("long may it wave," etc), was celebrated in this city with all that spirit and patriotism for which it has ever been distinguished.

Every citizen, with the exception of those who had retired in a state of intoxication, was aroused at 2 A.M. by the soul-stirring and tremendous report of the Plaza Artillery, which had been carefully loaded the previous evening with two pounds of powder and a half a bushel of public documents franked to this place by our late honorable representatives. Each citizen on being awakened in this manner (if he imitated the example of your respected reporter) reflected a moment with admiration on our glorious institutions; with pride on our great and increasing country, and with gratitude on the efforts of those patriotic spirits who had thus aroused him, and after murmuring some aspiration for their future happiness, was about to sink again to sleep, when — Bang! No. 2, more powder, more public documents, effectually aroused him again to go through the same train of thought, murmur the same aspirations, a little warmer, perhaps this time, and again become sleepy in time for Bang! No. 3. In this agreeable manner the attention was occupied, and the mind filled with patriotic ideas until just before daylight when the powder unfortunately gave out, though four bushels of public documents still remained (but they wouldn't go off) and the firing ceased. At sunrise the National Banner would have unfolded its "broad stripes and bright stars" to the breeze, but for the unlucky circumstances of there being no halliards to our flag-staff. We are gratified to learn that a new set will probably be furnished by the Board of Trustees before the next anniversary.

At 8 A.M. a procession was formed and moved to the sound of an excellent military band, consisting of a gong and a handbell, across the Plaza, where it separated into two divisions, one proceeding to the Union House, the other to the Colorado Hotel. At each of these excellent establishments an elegant *déjeuner* was served up, of the sumptuousness of which the following bill of fare will give some faint idea:

BREAKFAST BILL OF FARE

Coffee   Cafe, con sucre
Bread   Pan
Butter   Mantequilla
Friedbeefsteak Carne
Hash   No se

At 9 A.M., precisely, the San Diego Light Infantry in full uniform, consisting of Brown's little boy in his shirt-tail, fired a National salute with a large bunch of firecrackers. This part of the celebration went off admirably; with the exception of the young man having set fire to his shirt-tail, which was fortunately extinguished immediately, without incident.

At 12 P.M. an oration was delivered by a gentleman, in the Spanish language, in front of the Exchange, of which your reporter regrets to say he has been unable to remember but the concluding sentence, which, however, he is informed contains many fine ideas. It was nearly as follows:

"Hoy es el dia de Santa Refugia! (Hic) Los Americanos son abajos, no vale nada !(Hic) nada, nada, nada, (hiccup). Mira! Hombre, dar me poco de aguadiente Caramba!"

This oration was remarkably well received, and shortly after, the band commencing its performance, the procession was again formed, and dividing as before, moved off to dinner.

The afternoon passed pleasantly away in witnessing the performances of a gentleman who has been instituting a series of experiments to test the relative strength of various descriptions of spirituous liquor, and who becoming excited and enthusiastic thereby, walked around the Plaza and howled dismally.

Upon the whole, everything passed off in the most creditable manner, and we can safely say that never in our recollections have we witnessed *such* a celebration of the glorious anniversary of our Nation's Independence.

PIONEER MAGAZINE

The following parody appeared in the August, 1854 issue of *Pioneer Magazine*, California's first literary magazine, and was apparently inspired by a pretentious review in the *Pioneer* praising the production of *Le Desert-Ode Symphonie par Felicien David ,* which had recently opened at one of San Francisco's two grand theatres.

The *Pioneer* or *California Monthly Magazine* was patterned after the New York publication *Knickerbocker Magazine*, and was edited by Ferdinand C. Ewer, a visionary eccentric who somehow managed to publish the magazine without advertisements. Beginning with the magazine's first issue in January, 1854, Ewer published essays, poetry, correspondence from travelers such as the "Shirley Letters," and occassional satirical pieces.

In June, 1854, Lt. George Derby's first article appeared, and his John Phoenix contributions from the lonely outpost of San Diego were so funny that they attracted the attention of Thackeray in London and Lewis Gaylord Clark, editor of *Knickerbocker Magazine.* Derby's articles mocked San Francisco's pretentious theatre society, its literary reviews, and even its fleas. On a larger realm he attacked the Great Railroad Project and he spoofed the popularly-held belief in phrenology, the pseudo-scientific belief that the shape of one's head was a manifestation of character.

A MUSICAL REVIEW

First printed in the Pioneer, August, 1854

SAN DIEGO, **July 10, 1854.** AS YOUR valuable work is not supposed to be so entirely identified with San Franciscan interests as to be careless what takes place in other portions of this great *kedntry*, and as it is received and read in San Diego with great interest (I have loaned my copy to over four different literary gentlemen, most of whom have read some of it), I have thought it not improbable that a few critical notices of the musical performances and the drama of this place might be acceptable to you and interest your readers. I have been, moreover, encouraged to this task by the perusal of your interesting musical and theatrical critiques on San Francisco performers and performances; as I feel convinced that, if you devote so much space to them, you will not allow any little feeling of rivalry between the two great cities to prevent your noticing ours, which, without the slightest feeling of prejudice, I must consider infinitely superior. I propose this month to call your attention to the two great events in our theatrical and musical world — the appearance of the talented Miss Pelican, and the productions of Tarbox's celebrated Ode Symphonie of "The Plains."

The critiques on the former are from the columns of the Vallecitos *Sentinel*, to which they were originally contributed by me, appearing on the respective dates of June 1st and June 31st.

*From the Vallecitos **Sentinel**, June 1st.*

MISS PELICAN.— Never during our dramatic experience has a more exciting event occurred than the sudden bursting upon our theatrical firmament, full, blazing, unparalleled, of the bright, resplendent and particular star, whose honored name shines refulgent at the head of this article. Coming among us unheralded, almost unknown, without claptrap, in a wagon drawn by oxen across the plains, with no agent to set up a counterfeit enthusiasm in her favor, she appeared before us for the first time at the San Diego Lyceum, last evening, in the trying and difficult character of Ingomar, or the Tame Savage. We are at a loss to describe our sensations, our admiration, at her magnificent, her superhuman efforts. We do not hesitate to say that she is by far the superior of any living actress; and, as we believe hers to be the perfection of acting, we cannot be wrong in the belief that no one hereafter will ever be found to approach her. Her conception of the character of Ingomar was perfection itself; her playful and ingenuous manner, her light girlish laughter, in the scene with Sir Peter, showed an appreciation of the savage character which nothing but the most arduous study, the most elaborate training could produce; while her awful change to the stern, unyielding, uncompromising father in the tragic scene of Duncan's murder, was indeed nature itself. Miss Pelican is about seventeen years of age, of miraculous beauty, and most thrilling voice. It is needless to say she dresses admirably, as in fact we have said all we can say when we called her most truthfully, perfection. Mr. John Boots took the part of Parthenis very creditably, etc. etc..

Musical Review

*From the Vallecitos **Sentinel,** June 31st.*

> *MISS PELICAN — As this lady is about to leave us to commence an engagement on the San Francisco stage, we should regret exceedingly if any thing we have said about her should send with her a prestige which might be found undeserved on trial. The fact is, Miss Pelican is a very ordinary actress; indeed, one of the most indifferent ones we ever happened to see. She came here from the Museum at Fort Laramie, and we praised her so injudiciously that she became completely spoiled. She had performed a round of characters during the last week, very miserably, though we are bound to confess that her performance of King Lear last evening was superior to any thing of the kind we ever saw. Miss Pelican is about forty-three years of age, singularly plain in her personal appearance, awkward and embarassed, with a cracked and squeaking voice, and really dresses quite outrageously. She had much to learn, poor thing!*

I take it the above notices are rather ingenious. The fact is, I'm no judge of acting, and don't know how Miss Pelican will turn out. If well, why there's my notice of June the 1st. If ill, then June 31st comes in play, and, as there is but one copy of the *Sentinel* printed, it's an easy matter to destroy the incorrect one; *both can't be wrong*; so I've made a sure thing of it in any event. Here follows my musical critique, which I flatter myself is of rather superior order.

"THE PLAINS" ODE SYMPHONIE
PAR JABEZ TARBOX

This glorious composition was produced at the San Diego Odeon on the 31st of June, ult., for the first time in this or any other country, by a very full orchestra (the performance taking place immediately after supper), and a chorus composed of the entire "Sauer Kraut-Verein," the Wee Gates Association, and choice selections from the "Gyascutus" and "Pike-har-monic" societies. The solos were rendered by Herr Tuden Links, the recitations by Herr Von Hyden Schnapps, both performers being assisted by the Messrs. John Smith and Joseph Brown, who held their coats, fanned them, and furnished water during the more overpowering passages.

"The Plains" we consider the greatest musical achievement ever presented to an enraptured public. Like Waterloo among battles; Napoleon among warriors; Niagara among falls, and Peck among senators, this magnificent composition stands among Oratorios, Operas, Musical Melodramas and performances of Ethiopian Serenaders, peerless and unrivalled. *Il frappe toute chose parfaitment froid.*

It does not depend for its success upon its plot, its theme, its school or its master, for it has very little if any of them, but upon its soul-subduing, high-faluting effect upon the audience, every member of which it causes to experience the most singular and exquisite sensations. Its strains at times reminds us of those of the old master of the steamer *McKim*, who never went to sea without being unpleasantly affected — a straining after effect, he used to term it. Blair in his lecture on beauty, and Mills in his treatise on logic, (p. 31), have alluded to the feeling which might be produced in the human mind by something of this transcendentally sublime description, but it has remained for M. Tarbox, in the production of "The Plains," to call this feeling forth.

The symphonie opens upon the wide and boundless plains, in longitude 115 ° W., latitude 35 ° 21'03" N., and about sixty miles from the west bank of the Pitt River. These data are beautifully and clearly expressed by a long (topographically) drawn note from an E flat clarionet. The sandy nature of the soil, sparsely dotted with bunches of cactus and artemisia, the extended view, flat and unbroken to the horizon, save by the rising smoke in the extreme verge, denoting the vicinity of a Pi Utah village, are represented by a bass drum. A few notes on the piccolo calls the attention to a solitary antelope, picking up mescal beans in the foreground. The sun having an altitude of 36° 27', blazes down upon the scene in indescribable majesty. "Gradually the sounds roll forth in a song" of rejoicing to the God of Day.

> *Of thy intensity*
> *And great immensity*
> *Now then we sing;*
> *Beholding in gratitude*
> *Thee in this latitude,*
> *Curious thing.*

Which swells out into "Hey Jim along, Jim along Josey," then *decrescendo, mas o menos, poco pocita*, dies away and dries up.

Suddenly we hear approaching a train from Pike County, consisting of seven families with forty-six wagons, each drawn by thirteen oxen; each family consists of a man in butternut-colored clothing driving the oxen; a wife in butternut-colored clothing riding in the wagon, holding a butternut baby, and seventeen butternut children running promiscuously about the establishment; all are barefooted, dusty, and smell unpleasantly. (All these circumstances are expressed by pretty rapid fiddling for some minutes, winding up with a puff from the orpheclide, played by an intoxicated Teuton with an atrocious breath — it is impossible to misundertsand the description.) Now arises o'er the plains in mellifluous accents, the grand Pike County Chorus.

> *Oh we'll soon be thar*
> *In the land of gold*
> *Through the forest old,*
> *O'er the mounting cold,*
> *With spirits bold —*

Oh, we come, we come,
And we'll soon be thar.
Gee up Bolly! whoo, up, whoo haw!

The train now encamp. The unpacking of the kettles and
mess-pans, the unyoking of the oxen, the gathering about the
various camp-fires, the frizzling of the pork, are so clearly expressed by the music that the most untutored savage could
readily comprehend it. Indeed, so vivid and lifelike was the
representation, that a lady sitting near us involunatarily exclaimed aloud at a certain passage. *"Thar, that pork's burning!"* and it was truly interesting to watch the gratified
expression of her face when, by a few notes of the guitar, the
pan was removed from the fire and the blazing pork extinguished.

This is followed by the beautiful aria:

O! marm, I want a pancake!

Followed by that touching *recitative*:

Shet up, or I will spank you!

To which succeeds a grand crescendo movement, repre-
senting the flight of the child with the pancake, the pursuit of
the mother, and the final arrest and summary punishment of
the former, represented by the rapid and successive strokes of
the castanet.

The turning in for the night follows; and the deep and ster-
torous breathing of the encampment is well given by the bas-
soon, while the sufferings and trials of an unhappy father with
an unpleasant infant are touchingly set forth by the *cornet a
piston.*

Musical Review

Part Second.

The night attack of the Pi Utahs; the fearful cries of the
demoniac Indians; the shrieks of the females and children; the
rapid and effective fire of the rifles; the stampede of the oxen;
their recovery and the final repulse; the Pi Utahs being routed
after a loss of thirty-six killed and wounded, while the Pikes
lose but one scalp (from an old fellow who wore a wig and
lost it in the scuffle), are faithfully given, and excite the most
intense interest in the minds of the hearers; the emotions of
fear, admiration and delight succeeding each other in their
minds with almost painful rapidity. Then follows the grand
chorus:

Oh! we gin them fits,
The Ingen Utahs.
With our six-shooters —
We gin' em pertickuler fits.

After which we have the charming recitative of Herr Tuden
Links to the infant, which is really one of the most charming
gems of the performance:

Now, dern your skin, can't you be easy?

Morning succeeds. The sun rises magnificently (octavo
flute) — breakfast is eaten — in a rapid movement on three
sharps; the oxen are caught and yoked up, with a small drum
and triangle; the watches, purses, and other valuables of the
conquered Pi Utahs are stored away in a camp kettle, to a small
movement on the piccolo, and the train moves on, with the
grand chorus:

We'll soon be thar,
Gee up, Bolly! Whoo hup!, whoo haw!

The whole concludes with the grand hymn and chorus:

When we die we'll go to Benton,
Whup! Whoo, haw!
The greatest man that e'er land saw,
Gee!
Who this little airth was sent on
Whup! Whoo haw!
To tell a "hawk from a hand-saw!"
Gee!

The immense expense attending the production of this magnificent work; the length of time required to prepare the chorus; the incredible number of instruments destroyed at each rehearsal, have hitherto prevented M. Tarbox from placing it before the American public, and it had remained for San Diego to show herself superior to her sister cities of the Union, in musical taste and appreciation, and in high-souled liberality, by patronizing this immortal prodigy, and enabling its author to bring it forth in accordance with his wishes and its capabilities. We trust every citizen of San Diego and Vallecitos will listen to it ere it is withdrawn; and if there yet lingers in San Francisco one spark of musical fervor, or a remnant of taste for pure harmony, we can only say that the *Southerner* sails from that place once a fortnight and that the passage money is but forty-five dollars.

A NEW SYSTEM OF ENGLISH GRAMMAR*

First printed in the Pioneer, September, 1854

I HAVE OFTEN thought that the adjectives of the English language were not sufficiently definite for the purposes of description. They have but three degrees of comparison — a very insufficient number, certainly, when we consider that they are to be applied to a thousand objects, which, though of the same general class or quality, differ from each other by a thousand different shades or degrees of the same peculiarity. Thus, though there are three hundred and sixty-five days in a year, all of which must, from the nature of things, differ from each other in a matter of climate, we have but a half dozen expressions to convey to one another our ideas of this inequality. We say — "It's a fine day;" "It is a very fine day;" "It must

---

*Editors Note — Phrenology, the belief that the shape of the head was a manifestation of the character and brain, was very popular in the mid to late 1800's.

be the *finest* day we have seen;" or, "It is an unpleasant day;" "A *very* unpleasant day;" "The *most* unpleasant day we ever saw."

But it is plain that none of these expressions give an exact idea of the nature of the day; and the two superlative expressions are generally untrue. I once heard a gentleman remark, on a rainy, snowy, windy and (in the ordinary English language) indescribable day, that it was "most preposterous weather." He came nearer to giving a correct idea of it, than he could have done by any ordinary mode of expression; but his description was not sufficiently definite.

Again: we say of a lady — "She is beautiful;" "She is very beautiful," or "She is *perfectly* beautiful;" — descriptions which, to one who never saw her, are no descriptions at all, for among thousands of women he had seen, probably no two are equally beautiful; and as to a *perfectly* beautiful woman, he knows that no such being was ever created, unless G.P.R. James, for one of the two horsemen to fall in love with and marry at the end of the second volume.

If I meet Smith in the street and ask him, as I am pretty sure to do, "How he does?" He infallibly replies, "*Tolerable*, thank you," which gives me no *exact* idea of Smith's health, for he has made the same reply to me on a hundred different occasions — on every one of which there must have been some slight shade of difference in his physical economy, and of course a corresponding change in his feelings.

To a man of a mathematical turn of mind — to a student and lover of the exact sciences these inaccuracies of expression — this inability to understand *exactly* how things are, must be a constant source of annoyance; and to one who like myself, unites this turn of mind to an ardent love of truth, for its own sake, the reflection that the English language does not enable us to speak the truth with exactness, is peculiarly painful. For this reason I have, with some trouble, made myself thoroughly acquainted with every ancient and modern language, in the hope that I might find some one of them that would enable me to express precisely my ideas; but the same insufficiency of adjectives exists in all except that of the Flathead Indians of Puget Sound, which consists of but forty-six words, mostly nouns; but to the constant use of which exists the objection that nobody but that tribe can understand it. And as their literary and scientific advancement is not such as to make a residence among them, for a man of my disposition, desirable, I have abandoned the use of their language, in the belief that for me it is *hyas. cultus.*, or as the Spaniard hath it, *no me vale nada.*

Despairing, therefore, of making new discoveries in foreign languages, I have set myself seriously to work to reform our own; and have, I think, made an important discovery which, when developed into a system and universally adopted, will give a precision of expression, and a consequent clearness of idea, that will leave little to be desired, and will, I modestly hope, immortalize my humble name as the promulgator of the truth and the benefactor of the human race.

Before entering upon my system I will give you an account of its discovery (which perhaps I might with more modesty term an adaptation and enlargement of the idea of another) which will surprise you by its simplicity, and like the method of standing eggs on end, of Columbus, the inventions of printing, gunpowder and the mariner's compass, prove another exemplification of the truth of Hannah More's beautifully expressed sentiment:

Large streams from little fountains flow,

Large aches from little toe-corns grow.

During the past week my attention was attracted by a large placard embellishing the corners of our streets, headed in mighty capitals with the word "PHRENOLOGY," and illustrated by a map of a man's head, closely shaven, and laid off in lots, duly numbered from one to forty-seven. Beneath this edifying illustration appeared a legend, informing the inhabitants of San Diego and viciniy that Professor Dodge had arrived and taken rooms (which was inaccurate, as he had but one room) at the Gyascutus House, where he would be happy to examine and furnish them with a chart of their heads, showing the moral and intellectual endowments, at the low price of three dollars each.

Always gratified with an opportunity of spending my money and making scientific researches, I immediately had my hair cut and carefully combed, and hastened to present myself and my head to the Professor's notice. I found him a tall and thin Professor, in a suit of rusty, not to say seedy black, with a closely buttoned vest, and no perceptible shirt-collar or wristbands. His nose was red, his spectacles were blue, and he wore a brown wig, beneath which, as I subsequently ascertained, his bald head was laid off in lots, marked and numbered with Indian ink, after the manner of the diagram upon his advertisement. Upon a small table lay many little books with yellow covers, several of the placards, pen and ink, a pair of iron callipers with brass knobs, and six dollars in silver. Having explained the object of my visit, and increased the pile of silver by six half-dollars from my pocket — whereat he smiled, and I observed he wore false teeth — (scientific men always do; they love to encourage art) the Professor placed me in a chair, and rapidly manipulating my head, after the manner of a *sham pooh* (I am not certain as to the orthography of this expression), said that my temperament was "lymphatic, nervous, bilious." I remarked that I thought myself dyspeptic, but he made no reply. Then seizing on the callipers, he embraced with them my head in various places, and made notes upon a small card that lay near him on the table. He then stated that my hair was getting very thin on the top, placed in my hand one of the yellow-covered books, which I found to be an almanac containing anecdotes about the virtues of Dodge's Hair Invigorator, and recommending it to my perusal, he remarked that he was agent for the sale of this wonderful fluid, and urged me to purchase a bottle — price two dollars. Stating my willingness to do so, the Professor produced it from a hair trunk that stood in a corner of the room, which he stated, by the way, was originally an ordinary pine box, on which the hair had grown since the Invigorator had been placed in it, (a singular fact), and recommended me to be cautious in wearing gloves while rubbing in upon my head, as unhappy accidents had occurred — the hair growing freely from the ends of the fingers, if used with the bare hand. He then seated himself at the table, and rapidly filling up what appeared to me a blank certificate, he soon handed over the following singular document.

"Phrenological Chart of the head of M. John Phoenix, by Flatbroke B. Dodge, Professor of Phrenology, and inventor and proprietor of Dodge's celebrated Hair Invigorator, Stimulator of the Conscience, and Arouser of the Mental Faculties:

Temperament — *Lymphatic, Nervous, Bilious.*

Size of head, 11.	Imitation, 11.
Amativeness, 11 1/2.	Self-Esteem, 1/2.
Caution, 3.	Benevolence, 12.
Combativeness, 2 1/2.	Mirth, 1.
Credulity, 1.	Language, 12.
Causality, 12.	Firmness, 2.
Conscientiousness, 12.	Veneration, 12.
Destructiveness, 9.	Philoprogenitiveness, 0.
Hope, 10."	

Having gazed on this for a few moments in mute astonishment, during which the Professor took a glass of brandy and water, and afterwards a mouthful of tobacco, I turned to him and requested an explanation.

"Why," said he, "it's very simple; the number 12 is the maximum, 1 the minimum; for instance, you are as benevolent as a man can be — therefore I mark you Benevolence, 12. You have little or no self-esteem — hence I place you, Self-esteem, 1/2. You've scarcely any credulity, don't you see?"

I did see! This was my discovery. I saw at a flash how the English language was susceptible of improvement, and fired with the glorious idea, I rushed from the room and the house; heedless of the Professor's request that I would buy more of his Invigorator; heedless of his alarmed cry that I would pay for the bottle I'd got; heedless that I tripped on the last step of the Gyascutus House, and smashed there the precious fluid (the step has now a growth of four inches of hair on it, and the people use it as a door-mat); I rushed home, and never grew calm till with pen, ink and paper before me, I commenced the development of my system.

This system — shall I say this great system — is exceedingly simple, and easily explained in a few words. In the first place, "*figures won't lie.*" Let us then represent by the number 100, the maximum, the *ne plus ultra* of every human quality — grace, beauty, courage, strength, wisdom, learning — every thing. Let *perfection*, I say, be represented by 100, and an absolute minimum of all qualities by the number 1. Then by applying the numbers between, to the adjectives used in conversation, we shall be able to arrive at a very close approximation to the idea we wish to convey; in other words, we shall be enabled to speak the truth. Glorious, soul-inspiring idea!

For instance, the most ordinary question asked of you is, "How do you do?" To this, instead of replying, "Pretty well," "Very well," "Quite well," or the like absurdities — after running through your mind that *perfection* of health is 100, no health at all, 1 — you say, with a graceful bow, "Thank you, I'm 52 to-day;" or, feeling poorly, "I'm 13, I'm obliged to you," or "I'm 68," or "75," or "87 1/2," as the case may be! Do you see how very close in this way you may approximate to the truth; and how clearly your questioner will understand what he so anxiously wishes to arrive at — your *exact* state of health?

Let this system be adopted into our elements of grammar, our conversation, our literature, and we become at once an exact, precise, mathematical, truth-telling people. It will apply to every thing but politics; there, truth being of no account, the system is useless. But in literature, how admirable! Take an example:

"As a 19 young and 76 beautiful lady was 52 gaily tripping down the sidewalk of our 84 frequented street, she accidently come in contact 100 (this shows that she came in close contact) with a 73 fat, but 87 good-humored looking gentleman, who was 93 (i.e., intently) gazing into the window of a toy-shop. Gracefully 56 extricating herself, she received the excuses of the 96 embarrassed Falstaff with a 68 bland smile, and continued on her way. But hardly —7 —had she reached the corner of the block, ere she was overtaken by a 24 young man, 32 poorly dressed, but of an 85 expression of countenance; 91 hastily touching her 54 beautifully rounded arm, he said, to her 67 surprise,

"Madam, at the window of the toy-shop yonder, you dropped this bracelet, which I had the 71 good fortune to observe, and now have the 94 happiness to hand to you." (Of course the expression "94 happiness" is merely the young man's polite hyperbole.)

Blushing with 76 modesty, the lovely (76, as before, of course,) lady took the bracelet — which was a 24 magnificent diamond clasp — (24 *magnificent*, playfully sarcastic; it was

147

probably not one of Tucker's) from the young man's hand, and 84 hesitatingly drew from her beautifully 38 embroidered reticule a 67 port-monnaie. The young man noticed the action, and 73 proudly drawing back, added:

"Do not thank me; the pleasure of gazing for an instant at those 100 eyes (perhaps too exaggerated a compliment) has already more than compensated me for any trouble that I might have had."

She thanked him, however, and with a 67 deep blush and a 48 pensive air, turned from him, and pursued with a 33 slow step her promenade.

Of course you see that this is but the commencement of a pretty little tale, which I might throw off, if I had a mind to, showing in two volumes, or forty-eight chapters of thrilling interest, how the young man sought the girl's acquaintance, how the interest first excited, deepened into love, how they suffered much from the oppostion of parents (her parents, of course,) and how, after much trouble, annoyance, and many perilous adventures, they were finally married — their happiness, of course, being represented by 100. But I trust that I have said enough to recommend my system to the good and truthful of the literary world; and besides, just at present I have something of more immediate importance to attend to.

You would hardly believe it, but that everlasting (100) scamp of a Professor has brought a suit against me for stealing a bottle of his disgusting Invigorator; and as the suit comes off before a Justice of the Peace, whose only principle of law is to find guilty and fine any accused person whom he thinks has any money — (because if he don't, he has to take his costs in County Scrip), it behooves me to "take time by the forelock." So for the present, adieu. Should my system succeed to the extent of my hopes and expectations, I shall publish my new grammar early in the ensuing month, with suitable dedication and preface; and should you, with your well known liberality, publish my prospectus, and give me a handsome literary notice, I shall be pleased to furnish a presentation copy to each of the little *Pioneer* children.

P.S. I regret to add that having just read this article to Mrs. Phoenix, and asked her opinion thereon, she replied that "if a first-rate magazine article were represented by 100, she should judge this to be about 13; or if the quintessence of stupidity were 100, she should take this to be in the neighborhood of 96." This, as a criticism, is perhaps a little discouraging, but as an exemplification of the merits of my system it is exceedingly flattering. How could she, I should like to know, in ordinary language, have given so *exact* and truthful an idea — how expressed so forcibly her opinion (which, of course, differs from mine) on the subject?

As Dr. Samuel Johnson learnedly remarked to James Boswell, Laird of Auchinleck, on a certain occasion:

"Sir, the proof of the pudding is in the eating thereof."

ANTIDOTE FOR FLEAS

First Printed in the Pioneer, October, 1854

The following recipe from the writings of Miss Hannah More, may be found useful to your readers:

> *"In a climate where the attacks of fleas are a constant source of annoyance, any method which will alleviate them becomes a desideratum. It is therefore, with pleasure I make known the following recipe, which I am assured has been tried with efficacy.*
>
> *Boil a quart of tar until it becomes quite thin. Remove the clothing, and before the tar becomes perfectly cool, with a broad flat brush, apply a thin, smooth coating to the entire surface of the body and limbs. While the tar remains soft the flea becomes entangled in its tenacious folds, and is rendered perfectly harmless; but it will soon form a hard, smooth coating, entirely impervious to his bite. Should the coating crack at the knee or elbow joints, it is merely necessary to retouch it slightly at those places. The whole coat should be renewed every three or four weeks. This remedy is sure, and having the advantage of simplicity and economy, should be generally known."*

So much for Miss More. A still simpler method of preventing the attacks of these little pests, is one which I have lately discovered myself — in theory only — I have not yet put it into practice. On feeling the bite of a flea, thrust the part bitten immediately into boiling water. The heat of the water destroys the insect and instantly removes the pain of the bite.

You have probably heard of old Parry Dox. I met him here a few days since, in a sadly seedy condition. He told me that he was still extravagantly fond of whisky, though he was constantly "running it down."

I inquired after his wife.

"She is dead, poor creature," said he, "and is probably far better off than ever she was here. She was a seamstress, and her greatest enjoyment of happiness in this world was only so, so."

A LEGEND OF THE

TEHAMA HOUSE,
Corner of California and Sansome Streets.

THIS WELL KNOWN AND POPULAR
Establishment offers superior inducements to
the traveling Public, and to those wishing a quiet home.
It is situated in convenient proximity to the business
centre, and is conducted on the European plan, giving
its patrons the choice of obtaining their meals at the
Restaurant connected with the house, or elsewhere, as
their convenience may suggest.
The Proprietor, who has been engaged in this house
since 1852, solicits a continuance of the patronage of his
many friends, which, as heretofore, he will endeavor to
merit by strict attention to their wants and comfort.
mh24   G. W. FRINK, Proprietor.

TEHAMA HOUSE

First printed in the Pioneer, December 1854

CHAPTER I

It was evening at the Tehama. The apothecary, whose shop
formed the southeastern corner of that edifice, had lighted
his lamps, which shining through those large glass bottles in
the window, filled with red and blue liquors, once supposed
by this author, when young and innocent, to be medicine of
the most potent description, lit up the faces of the passersby
with an unearthly glare, and exaggerated the general redness
and blueness of their noses. Within the office the hands of the
octagonal clock, which looked as though it had been thrown
against the wall in a moist state and stuck there, pointed to the
hour of eight. The apartment was nearly deserted. Frink, "the
courteous and gentlemanly manager,"and the Major had gone

to the theatre — having season tickets they felt themselves forced to attend and never missed a performance. The coal fire in the office stove glowed with a hospitable warmth, emitting a gentle murmur of welcome to the expected wayfarers by the Sacramento boats, interrupted only by an occasional deprecatory hiss, when insulted by a stream of tobacco juice. Overcoats hung about the walls, still moist with recent showers; umbrellas reclined lazily in corners; spittoons stood about the floor, the whole diffusing that nameless odor so fascinating to the married man, who, cigar in mouth and hot whiskey punch at elbow, sits nightly until twelve o'clock in the enjoyment of it, while the wife of his bosom in their comfortable home on Powell Street, wonders at his absence, and unjustly curses the Know Nothings or the Free and Accepted Masonic Fraternity.

Behind the office desk, perched on a high, three-legged stool, his head supported by both hands, the youthful but literary John Duncan was deeply engaged in the exciting perusal of the last yellow-colored novel, *Blood for Blood, or the Infatuated Dog*. He knew that, in a few moments, eighty-four gentlemen "in hot haste" would call to inquire whether the Member of Congress had returned, and was anxious to find out what the "Robber Chieftain" did with the "Lady Maude Alleyne" before the arrival of the Sacramento boat. The only other occupant of the office was a short, fleshy gentleman with a white hat, dark green coat with brass buttons, drab pantaloons, short punchy little boots and gaiters.

These circumstances might be noted as he stood with his back to the door, gazing intently upon one of those elaborate works of art with which the spirited proprietor has lately seen fit to adorn the walls of the Tehama. It represented a lady in a ball dress, seated on the back of a large dray-horse (at least eighteen hands high), and holding a parrot on her right forefinger, while at her horse's feet kneeled a man in the stage dress of Mercutio, doing something with five or six other parrots. The piece was called "Hawking," had a fine gilt frame and glass, and in certain lights, answered the purpose of a mirror; and was therefore a very pretty object to gaze upon. In fact, the short, stout gentleman was adjusting his shirt collar, which was of prodigious height, and had a perverse inclination to turn down on one side, by its reflection.

As he turned from his employment, he exhibited one of the most curious faces it is possible to conceive. Unlike most fat men, whose little eyes, round, red cheeks, wart-like noses and double chins, convey but little meaning or expression, this gentleman's face was all expression. He wore a constant look of the most intense curiosity. Inquisitiveness sat upon every lineament of his countenance. His small, green eyes protruding from his head, surmounted by thin but well-defined and very curvilinear eyebrows, looked like two notes of interrogation; his nose, though small, was sharp at the end like a gimlet, and his little round mouth was constantly pursed up into an expression of inquiring wonder, as though the most natural sound that could fall from it should be, "O-o-o-o! Come now, do tell."

In fact he was one of those beings created by a wise but inscrutable Providence for no other purpose apparently but "to meddle with other people's business," and ask questions.

His name was Bogle, and with Mrs. Bogle, whom he had married two years before, because, having exhausted all other subjects of inquiry in conversation with her, he had finally asked her if she would have him, and a little Bogle, who had made its appearance some three months since, and already "took notice" with an inquiring air painful to contemplate, he occupied for the present Room No. 31.

Bogle would have made a fortune in no time if he had lived in the blessed era when the promise "Ask and ye shall receive" was fulfilled; and so well was his disposition understood by the frequenters of the Tehama that they invariably left the vicinity when he looked askant at them; his presence cleared the room as quickly as a stream from a fire engine, or a mad dog could have done it.

Brushing some remains of snuff from his snow-white vest (Bogle took snuff inordinately) he turned upon the hapless Duncan, who had just got the Lady Maude into the cave where the skeleton hand dripped blood from the ceiling: "John, what time is it?"

John looked at the clock with a slight groan, "Five minutes past eight, Mr. Bogle."

"What time will the boat be in?"

"In a few moments, Mr. Bogle."

"Will the General come down tonight?"

"I don't know, Mr. Bogle."

"How old a man do you take him to be now?"

"'Fontaine, she screamed!' — that is, I don't know, Mr. Bogle."

"How much does he weigh?"

"The skeleton! Indeed, I don't know, sir."

The conversation was here suspended by the sudden arrival of a stranger. He was a large man, of stern and forbidding aspect, exceedingly dark complexion, with long, black hair hanging in unkempt tangles about his shoulders, and with a fierce and uncompromising moustache and beard, blacker than the driven charcoal, completely concealing the lower part of his face. His dress was singular; a brown hat, brown coat, brown vest, brown neck-cloth, brown pantaloons, brown gaiter boots. In his hand he carried a brown carpet-bag, and beneath his arm a brown silk umbrella. Hastily he inscribed his name upon the register, "General Tecumseh Brown, Brownsville," and for an instant seemed to fall into a brown study. Bogle was on the *qui vive;* he looked over the General's shoulder.

"From Sacramento, sir?" said he.

The general gazed at Bogle sternly for a moment, and replied, "I am, sir."

"I see, sir," said Bogle with a cordial smile, "you live in Brownsville; may I inquire if you are in business there?"

The general gazed at Bogle more sternly than before, and shortly answered, "You may, sir."

"Well," said Bogle, "are you?"

"Yes, sir," replied General Brown in a stentorian voice, at the same time advancing a step toward his fat little inquisitor, "I have lately made a fortune there."

"Oh!" said Bogle, nimbly jumping back as the General advanced, "How?"

"*By minding my own business, sir!*" thundered the General, and turning to Duncan, who had forgotten the Lady Maude in the charms of this conversation, said, "Give me my key, sir, and the moment a young man calls here to inquire for me, send him up to my room."

So saying, and grasping the key extended to him, General Brown turned away, and casting a look of fierce malignity at little Bogle, who tried to conceal his confusion by taking a pinch of snuff, retired, taking with him as he went the only brown japanned candlestick that stood among the numerous arrays of those articles, provided for the Tehama's guests.

"Well," said Bogle, "of all the Brown — where did you put him, John?"

"No. 32," replied that individual, returning to "the cave."

"Thirty-two!" exclaimed Bogle, "goodness gracious! Why that joins my room, and the partition is as thin as a wafer."

CHAPTER II

Upstairs went Bogle, two steps at a time. The door of thirty-two slammed as he reached the door of his apartment; it slammed on a brown coat-tail, about half a yard of which remained on the outside; there was a muttered ejaculation, then a deep growl, and rip! went the coat-tail, the fragment remaining on the door.

"Gracious! Goodness!" said Bogle, "what a passionate man! He's torn it off! He's like Alley's comet; no! That never had a tail! He's like that fox," — and Bogle entered his apartment.

Here sat his interesting wife, rocking their offspring, and instilling into its infant mind the first lesson of practical economy by singing that popular nursery refrain,

Buy low, Baby; Buy low, buy low.

"Hush!" said Bogle as he entered on tip-toe, and carefully closed the door of thirty-one, held up a warning finger to the partner of his joys and sorrows. The lullaby ceased. It is said that all women become like their husbands after a certain time, both in appearance and disposition. Mrs. Bogle, who had been a Miss Artemesia Stackpole before marriage (Bogle said she was named for an elder sister, Mesia, who died, and she was called Arter-mesia), certainly did not at all resemble her husband in appearance. She was of the thread-paper order; one of those gaunt, bony females of no particular age, who always have two false eye-teeth, and wear brown merino dresses and muslin night-caps with a cotton lace border in the morning. But in disposition she was his very counterpart. Curious, meddling, inquisitive, fond of gossip and indefatigable in "the pursuit of knowledge under difficulties," she was an invaluable coadjutor to Bogle, whom she has materially assisted many times in obtaining information that even his prying nature had failed to accomplish. Eagerly she listened to his tale about the mysterious Brown and *his* tail, and like a good and dutiful wife, all quietly she nursed the olive branch, while Bogle, seated in close proximity to the partition, listened with eager ear, intent, to the motions of their neighbor.

Three times in as many quarters of an hour did that mysterious General ring the bell; three times came up the waiter; three times he replied to the General's anxious question, "that no one had called for him," and three times he went down again. After each interview with the waiter, Bogle, listening at the partition, heard the General mutter to himself a large word, a scriptual word, but not adapted to common conversation; it began with a capital **D** and ended with a small **n**. Each time that he heard it, Bogle said "Gracious! Goodness!"

At length his patient exertions were rewarded. As the clock struck ten, a step was heard upon the stairs; nearer and nearer it came. Bogle's heart beat heavily; it stopped in front of thirty-two; he held his breath — a knock — the General's voice, "Come in;" — he heard the door open and the stranger commence with "Good evening, General —" but before he could say "Brown," that gentleman exclaimed, "Charles, *have* you seen Fanny?"

Bogle, his ear glued to the wall, turned his eye toward his wife and beckoned. Artemesia approached, and seating herself on his knee, the infant clasped to her breast, listened with her husband.

The stranger slowly replied, "I have."

"And who was she with?"

"That Frenchman, as you supposed."

"Good God!" exclaimed the stricken Brown, as in agony he paced the room in fearful strides. There was a moment's silence.

"Did you take her from him?"

"Yes, I persuaded her to accompany me to my room at The Union.

"Why did you not bring her to me at once?"

"I knew your passionate nature, General, and I feared you would kill her."

"I *will*" growled the General, "By Heaven, I will! — but not so! — not as you think; I'll poison her!"

Bogle, his face pallid with apprehension, his teeth chattering with fear, looked at Artemesia; she met his horror-

stricken gaze, and with a subdued shriek, clasped the baby —
it awoke.

The General, in a low, deep voice of concentrated passion,
continued; "I'll poison her, Charles!"

"Oh!" he exclaimed with deep emotion, "how I have loved
that —"

Here the infant Bogle, who had been drawing in his breath
for a cry, broke forth; "At once there rose so wild a yell —"
Human nature could not stand it any longer.

"Smother that little villain!" said Bogle in a fierce whisper;
"I can't hear a word."

Artemesia, with a look of Lucretia Borgia, withdrew with
the child to the adjoining room (No. 31, Tehama, contains two
rooms, a small parlor and a bed-chamber), and administered a
punishment that must have astonished it — it was certainly
struck aback. If babies remember anything, that youthful
Bogle has not forgotten that bastinado — applied a little higher
up than is customary among the Turks — to this day. "At
length the tumult dwindled to a calm," and again Bogle
clapped his ear to the wall. He heard but the concluding words
of the murderous General:

"Bring her up with you at ten o'clock to-morrow evening,
and a sack; after it is over, we will put her body in it. and carry
her to Meigg's wharf, where there are plenty of brick; we can
fill the sack with them and throw her off."

"Well, sir," replied the stranger, "if you are determined to
do it, I will; but poor Fanny!" — here emotion choked his utterance.

"You do as I tell you, sir;" growled the General, "there's no
weakness about me!" here the door opened and closed.

Bogle rose from his knees, the perspiration was running
down his face in streams.

"No weakness," said he, "Goodness! Gracious! I should
say not. What an awful affair. Coming so close, too, upon the
Meiggs forgeries, and the loss of the Yankee Blade. How

providential that I happened to overhear it all! Gracious, Goodness!"

That night, in a whispered consultation with his Artemesia, Bogle's plan of action was decided upon. But long after this, and long after the horror-stricken pair had sunk into a perturbed slumber, the footsteps of the intended murderer might have been heard, as hour after hour he paced the floor of his solitary chamber, and his deep voice might have been heard also, occasionally giving vent to his fell determination —

"Yes, *sir!* I'll — **mur-der**!!!!—!!!!—!!!—!"

CHAPTER III

The next morning a great change might have been observed in our friend Bogle. He appeared unusually quiet and reserved — pallid and nervous — starting when anyone approached him, he stood alone near the door of the Tehama; he sought no companionship, he asked no questions. Men marvelled thereat.

"What has come over Bogle?" asked the Judge to the Major. "I haven't heard him ask a question today."

"Well," was the unfeeling reply, "he's been asking questions for the last thirty years, and I reckon he's asked all there are."

But Bogle knew what he was about. At three P.M. precisely, General Brown came majestically down the stairs; he passed Bogle so nearly that he could have touched him; but he noticed not the latter's shuddering withdrawal; he looked neither to the right or left, but, gloomy and foreboding, like an avenging genius, he passed into the apothecary's on the corner.

"Give me an ounce bottle of strychnine," he said.

"For rats, sir?" said the polite attendant.

The General started; he gave a fearful scowl. "Yes," he said with a demoniac laugh, "for rats Ha! Ha! Oh, yes — for — rats!"

Bogle heard this; he heard no more; he started for the Police Office.

Who was Fanny? — ?? — ????! — ?—???

That evening about ten o'clock, Bogle sat alone, or alone save his Artemesia, in No. 31. The baby had been put to bed; and silent and solemn in that dark apartment, for the lamp had been extinguished, sat listening that shuddering pair. A step was heard on the stairs, and closer drew the Bogles together, listening to that step, as it sounded fearfully distinct from the beating of their own agitated hearts.

As it drew near, it was evident that two persons were approaching; for, accompanying the first distinct tread, was a light footfall like that of a young and tender female. "Poor thing!" said Artemesia, with a suppressed gasp. The heavy tread of General Brown could be heard distinctly in No. 32. The parties stopped at his door; a knock, and they were silently admitted.

The voice of the General broke the silence — "Oh! Fanny," he exclaimed in bitter anguish, "how could you desert me!" There was no articulate reply, but the Bogles heard from the unhappy female an expression of grief, which almost broke their hearts.

"Fanny," continued the General, "you have been faithless to me — fickle and false as your sex invariably are! I loved you Fanny — I love you still! — but my heart can no more be made the sport of falsehood! You must die! Take this!"

"Hold, wretch!" shouted Bogle. "Let me go, Artemesia;" and throwing off his coat, the heroic little fellow threw open his own door, kicked down the door of thirty-two and stood in the presence of the murderer and his victim, pistol in hand!

At the same instant the bell of thirty-one was violently rung, the doors on each side opened, and the gallery was filled with men. But what caused Bogle to falter? Why did he not rush forward to snatch the victim from her destroyer? Near the centre-table, on which was burning an astral lamp, stood a remarkably fine looking young man, who gazed on Bogle's short, paunchy figure with an inquiring smile.

On the other side of the table, but nearer the door, his brow blacker than a thunder-cloud, sat General Brown; in one hand he held a small piece of meat, the other retained between his knees a small but exceedingly stanch-looking dog, of the true bull-terrier breed. Both the General and the dog showed their teeth; both were epitomes of ferocity, but the snarl of the dog was nothing to the snarl of the General, as, half-rising from his seat, but still holding the dog down by the collar, he shouted: "How's this, sir?"

Bogle staggered back — dashing back from his brow the perspiration, he dropped the pistol and leaning against the door, gasped rather than articulated: "It's a dog!"

"Yes, sir!" roared the infuriated General, rising from his chair, "*and a she dog at that*! What have *you* got to say about it?"

Bogle, almost fainting, stammered painfully forth, "Is her — name — Fanny?"

"D—n you, sir," screamed the General, "I'll let you know! Sta-boy! Bite him, Fan."

Like an arrow from a bow, like a lightning from the cloud, like shot off a shovel, like anything that goes quick, sprang the female bull-terrier on the unhappy Bogle.

"Man is but mortal," and Bogle turned to flee. "It was too late!" Why did he take off his coat? — Ah! Why wear such tight pantaloons?

Shrieking like a demon, the ferocious beast clinging to one extremity, his hair on end with fright and horror at the other, Bogle rushed frantically down the passage, overturning in his mad career, police officers, chambermaids, housekeeper and boarders, who, alarmed at his outcries, thronged tumultuously into the hall. The first flight of stairs he took at a jump; the second he rolled down from top to bottom, the bull-terrrier clinging to him like a steel trap — first the dog on top, then Bogle; arrived at the bottom, he sprang forth into Sansome Street, and reckless of Frink's alarmed cry — "Stop that man — he hasn't paid his bill!" away he went on the wings of the wind. It was an awful sight to see that little figure as, wild with horror, he ran adown the street, the stanch dog swinging from side to side, as he fled.

It was a fearful race! Never did a short pair of legs get over an equal space in an equal time, than on that trying occasion. At length a sailor on Commercial Street, taking the dog for a portmanteau, with which he supposed Bogle was making off, stretched out a friendly leg and tripped him up. But his troubles were not ended. When a bull-terrier takes a hold — a fair hold — to get him off, one of two alternatives must obtain; either the animal's teeth must be drawn, or the piece must come out. They hadn't time to draw Fanny's teeth!

They brought Bogle home in a hand-cart, and put him to bed. He hasn't sat down since. As they took him upstairs to his room, surrounded by a clamorous throng, the door of No. 10, at the foot of the first flight of stairs, opened, and a gentleman of exceeding dignity made his appearance in a dressing gown of beautifully embroidered pattern.

"John," he said to Mr. Duncan, who, with an extensive grin on his countenance, and "Blood for Blood" (somewhat dilapidated in the scuffle) in his hand, was bringing up the rear of the procession with a candle, "what's all this row about?"

John briefly explained.

"I thought it a fire," said the gentleman, "but, *Parturiunt montes, nascetur* —"

"A ridiculous mess," said the classic John Duncan.

The gentleman retired; so did the chambermaid; so did the boarders generally; so did General Brown, with his dog under his arm, swearing he would not part with her for five hundred dollars; so did the policemen, somewhat scandalized that nobody was murdered after all.

Bogle left the house next day in a baby-jumper, swung to a pole between two Chinamen. Artemesia and the infant followed.

I hear that he has lately increased his business, taken a partner, and attended to the examination of wills, marriage settlements, and other papers belonging entirely to other people's business. Sneak is the name of the partner; he or Bogle may be seen daily at the Hall of Records, from ten until two o'clock, over-hauling something or other, that is no concern of theirs. They furnish all sorts of information *gratis*. It is like the wine you get where they advertise "All sorts of liquors at 12 1/2 cents a glass."

General Brown has settled in Grass Valley, Nevada County, and would have appointed every white male inhabitant of California a member of his staff with the rank of lieutenant-colonel, had he not been anticipated.

Fanny killed forty-four rats in thirty seconds, only last week — so Tom says.

The Tehama House is still there.

On September 24, 1854, Derby wrote a bitter letter to Colonel Abert requesting a transfer from San Diego.

> *It may appear that as I have been doing nothing here for a year, I have not much reason to expect indulgence, ... but I can assure you that an exile to this dreary and desolate little place, with nothing whatever to do, is about the most disagreeable duty that I could possibly have performed.*

Derby was not pleased with the direction of his "professional" army career. 1853-1854 were the years of the Great Pacific Railroad survey, and most of Derby's comrades from the Topographical Corps had been dispatched to survey the proposed transcontinental railroad. Derby had hoped for an appointment as surveyor on the The Great Railroad project, but instead of charting the wilderness, in November, 1854, Derby was ordered to report as aide-de-camp to General Wool, headquartered in San Francisco.

The Derbys arrived in San Francisco in time for Mary to deliver their first child, Daisy Peyton Derby, on December 3, 1854. Dr. Charles Hitchcock, the engineer's surgeon friend from West Point, was the child's godfather. Unlike Dr. Hitchcock, who had become rich with his real estate investments, Derby found that he could no longer afford to live in bustling San Francisco on a second lieutenant's salary, and the family settled into a tiny shack in the Mission District.

At $89.83 a month, his salary was a joke — especially in a city where a basket of strawberries cost 75 cents — but Derby's position as an aide-de-camp was a sinecure, and soon the trouble-maker lieutenant turned his focus on the Great Railroad Survey, a project which was on everyone's lips at the time. When the young Derby explored the Sierras in July, 1849 he had only a rusty compass to guide him, yet the greenhorn surveyors on the new Railroad Project carried transits, repeating revolvers, and barometers. Derby spoofed the blunders and pomposity of the well-supplied Great Railroad Project in the following article for *Pioneer.*

OFFICIAL REPORT OF PROFESSOR JOHN PHOENIX

*Of a Military Survey & Reconnoisance of the route from San Francisco to the Mission of Dolores, made with a view to ascertain the practicability of connecting these points by a Railroad.**

First printed in the Pioneer, March, 1855.

Mission of Dolores, **February 15, 1855.** It having been definitely determined that the great Railroad, connecting the City of San Francisco with the head of navigation on Mission Creek, should be constructed without unnecessary delay, a large appropriation ($120,000) was granted, for the purpose of causing thorough military examinations to be made of the proposed routes. The routes which had principally attracted the attention of the public were "the Northern," following the line of Brannan Street, "the Central," through Folsom Street, and "the extreme Southern," passing over the "Old Plank Road" to the Mission. Each of these proposed routes has many enthusiastic advocates; but "the Central" was, undoubtedly, the favorite of the public, it being more extensively used by emigrants from San Francisco to the Mission and therefore more widely and favorably known than the

---

*The Mission Dolores is only 2 1/2 miles from the City Hall of San Francisco, and is a favorite suburban locality, lying within the limits of the City Survey. This fact is noted for the benefit of distant readers of these sketches.

others. It was to the examination of this route that the Committee, feeling a confidence (eminently justified by the result of my labors) in my experience, judgment and skill as a Military Engineer, appointed me on the first instant. Having notified that honorable body of my acceptance of the important trust confided in me, in a letter, wherein I also took occasion to congratulate them on the good judgment they had evinced, I drew from the Treasurer the amount ($40,000) appropriated for my peculiar route, and having invested it securely in loans at three per cent a month (made to avoid accident in my own name), I proceeded to organize my party for the expedition.

In a few days my arrangements were completed, and my scientific corps organized, as follows:

John Phoenix, A.M.	*Principal Engineer and Chief Astronomer*
Lieut. Minus Root	*Apocryphal Engineers, First Assistant Astronomer*
Lieut. Nonplus A. Zero	*Hypercritical Engineers, Second Assistant Astronomer*
Dr. Abraham Dunshunner	*Geologist*
Dr. Targee Heavysterne	*Naturalist*
Herr Von Der Weegates	*Botanist*
Dr. Fogy L. Bigguns	*Ethnologist*
Dr. Tushmaker	*Dentist*
Enry Halfred Jinkins, R.A.	*Draftsman*
Adolphe Kraut	*Draftsman*
Hi Fun	*Interpreter*
James Phoenix (my elder brother)	*Treasurer*
Joseph Phoenix (ditto)	*Quarter-Master*
William Phoenix (younger brother)	*Commissary*
Peter Phoenix (ditto)	*Clerk*
Paul Phoenix (my cousin)	*Sutler*
Reuben Phoenix (ditto)	*Wagon-Master*
Richard Phoenix (second cousin)	*Assistant ditto*

These gentlemen, with one hundred and eighty-four laborers employed as teamsters, chainmen, rodmen, etc., made up the party. For instruments we had 1 large Transit Instrument (8 inch acromatic lens), 1 Mural Circle, 1 Altitude and Azimuth Instrument (these instruments were permanently set up in a mule cart which was backed into the plane of the true meridian when required for use), 13 large Theodolites, 13 small ditto, 8 Transit Compasses, 17 sextants, 34 Artificial Horizons, 1 Sidereal Clock, and 184 Solar Compasses. Each employee was furnished with a gold chronometer watch, and, by a singular mistake, a diamond pin and gold chain; for directions having been given that they should be furnished with *"chains and pins,"* — meaning of course such articles as are used in surveying — Lieut. Root, whose "zeal somewhat overran his discretion," incontinently procured for each man the above-named articles of jewelry, by mistake. They were purchased at Tucker's (where, it is needless to remark, "you can buy a diamond pin or ring"), and afterwards proved extremely useful in our intercourse with the natives of the Mission of Dolores, and indeed along the route.

Every man was suitably armed with four of Colt's revolvers, a Minie rifle, a copy of Col. Benton's speech on the Pacific Railroad, and a mountain howitzer. These last-named heavy articles required each man to be furnished with a wheelbarrow for their transportation, which was accordingly done; and these vehicles proved of great service on the survey, in transporting not only the arms but the baggage of the party, as well as the plunder derived from the natives. A squadron of dragoons, numbering 150 men, under Capt. McSpadden, had been detailed as an escort. They accordingly left about a week before us, and we heard of them occasionally on the march.

On consulting with my assistants, I had determined to select as a base for our operations a line joining the summit of Telegraph Hill with the extremity of the wharf at Oakland, and two large iron thirty-two pounders were accordingly procured and at great expense imbedded in the earth, one at each extremity of the line, to mark the initial points. On placing compasses over these points to determine the bearing of the base, we were extremely perplexed by the unaccountable local attraction that prevailed; and were compelled, in consequence, to select a new position. This we finally concluded to adopt between Fort Point and Saucelito; but on attempting to measure the base, we were deterred by the unexpected depth of the water intervening, which, to our surprise, was considerably over the chainbearers' heads. Disliking to abandon our new line, which had been selected with much care and at great expense, I determined to employ in its measurement a reflecting instrument, used very successfully by the United States Coast Survey. I therefore directed my assistants to procure me a "Heliotrope," but after being annoyed by having brought to me successively a sweet-smelling shrub of that name, and a box of "Lubin's Extract" to select from, it was finally ascertained that no such instrument could be procured in California. In this extremity I bethought myself of using as a substitute the flash of gunpowder. Wishing to satisfy myself of its practicability by an experiment, I placed Dr. Dunshunner at a distance of forty paces from my Theodolite, with a flint-lock musket carefully primed, and directed him to flash in the pan when I should wave my hand. Having covered the Doctor with the Theodolite, and by a movement of the tangent screw placed the intersection of the cross lines directly over the muzzle of the musket, I accordingly waved; when I was astounded by a tremendous report, a violent blow in the eye, and the instantaneous disappearance of the instrument.

Observing Dr. Dunshunner lying on his back in one direction, and my hat, which had been violently torn from my head, at about the same distance in another, I concluded that the musket had been accidentally loaded. Such proved to be the case; the marks of three buckshot were found in my hat, and a shower of screws, broken lenses and pieces of brass which shortly fell around us, told where the ball had struck, and bore fearful testimony to the accuracy of Dr. Dunshunner's practice. Believing these experiments more curious than useful, I abandoned the use of the "Heliotrope" or its substitutes, and determined to reverse the usual process, and arrive at the length of the base line by subsequent triangulation. I may as well state here that this course was adopted and resulted to our entire satisfaction; the distance from Fort Point to Saucelito by the solution of a mean of 1,867,434,926,465 triangles being determined to be exactly *three hundred and twenty-four feet*. This result differed very much from our preconceived ideas and from the popular opinion; the distance being generally supposed to be some ten miles; but I will stake my professional reputation on the accuracy of our work and there can, of course, be no disputing the elucidations of science, or facts demonstrated by mathematical process, however incredible they may appear *per se*.

We had adopted an entire new system of triangulation, which I am proud to claim (though I hope with becoming modesty) as my own invention. It simply consists in placing one leg of a tripod on the initial point, and opening out the other legs as far as possible; the distance between the legs is then measured by a two-foot rule and noted down; and the tripod moved so as to form a second triangle, connected with the first, and so on until the country to be triangulated has been entirely gone over. By using a large number of tripods, it is easily seen with what rapidity the work may be carried on, and this was, in fact, the object of my requisition for so large a number of solar compasses, the tripod being in my opinion the only useful portion of that absurd instrument. Having given Lieut. Root charge of the triangulation, and detached Mr. Jinkins with a small party on hydrographical duty (to sound a man's well on the upper part of Dupont Street and report thereon), on the 5th of February I left the Plaza, with the *savans* and the remainder of my party, to commence the examination and survey of **Kearny Street.**

Besides the mules drawing the cart which carried the transit instrument, I had procured two fine pack mules, each of which carried two barrels of ale for the draftsmen. Following the tasteful example of that gallant gentleman who conducted the Dead Sea Expedition, and wishing likewise to pay a compliment to the administration under which I was employed, I named the mules Fanny Pierce and Fanny Bigler. Our *cortege* passing along Kearny Street attracted much attention from the natives, and indeed, our appearance was sufficiently imposing to excite interest even in less untutored minds than those of these barbarians.

First came the cart, bearing our instruments; then a cart containing Lieut. Zero with a level, with which he constantly noted the changes of grade that might occur; then one hundred and fifty men, four abreast, armed to the teeth, each wheeling before him his personal property and a mountain howitzer; then the *savans*, each with note-book and pencil, constantly jotting down some object of interest (Doctor Tushmaker was so zealous to do something that he pulled a tooth from an iron rake standing near a stable-door, and was cursed therefor by the illiberal proprietor), and finally the Chief Professor, walking arm in arm with Dr. Dunshunner, and gazing from side to side, with an air of ineffable blandness and dignity, brought up the rear.

I had made arrangements to measure the length of Kearny Street by two methods; first, by chaining its sidewalks, and secondly, by a little instrument of my invention called the "Go-it-ometer." This last consists of a straight rod of brass, firmly strapped to a man's leg and connected with a system of clock-work placed on his back, with which it performs, when he walks, the office of a *ballistic pendulum*. About one foot below the ornamental buttons on the man's back appears a dial-plate connected with the clock-work, on which is promptly registered, by an index, each step taken. Of course, the length of the step being known, the distance passed over in a day may be obtained by a very simple process.

We arrived at the end of Kearny Street and encamped for the night about sundown, near a large brick building inhabited by a class of people called "The Orphans," who, I am credibly informed, have no fathers or mothers! After seeing the camp properly arranged, the wheelbarrows parked and a guard detailed, I sent for the chainmen and "Go-it-ometer" bearer, to ascertain the distance travelled during the day.

Judge of my surprise to find that the chainmen, having received no instructions, had simply drawn the chain after them through the streets, and had no idea of the distance whatever. Turning from them in displeasure, I took from the "Go-it-ometer" the number of paces marked, and on working the distance, found it to be four miles and a half. Upon close questioning the bearer, William Boulder (called by his associates "Slippery Bill"), I ascertained that he had been in a saloon in the vicinity, and after drinking five glasses of a beverage known among the natives as *Lager Bier*," he had danced a little for their amusement. Feeling very much dissatisfied with the day's survey, I stepped out of the camp, and stopping an omnibus, asked the driver how far he thought it to the Plaza? He replied, "Half a mile," which I accordingly noted down and returned very much pleased at so easily obtaining so much valuable information. It would appear, therefore, that Slippery Bill, under the influence of five glasses (probably 2 1/2 quarts) of "*Lager Bier*," had actually danced four miles in a few moments.

Kearny Street, of which I present above a spirited engraving from a beautiful drawing by Mr. Kraut, is a pass about fifty feet in width. The soil is loose and sandy, about one inch in depth, below which Dr. Dunshunner discovered a stratum of white pine three inches in thickness, and beneath this again, sand.

It is densely populated, and smells of horses. Its surface is intersected with many pools of *sulphuretted protoxide of hydrogen,* and we found several specimens of a vegetable substance, loosely distributed, which is classed by Mr. Weegates as the *stalkus cabbagiensis.*

It being late in the evening when our arrangements for encamping were completed, we saw but little of the natives until the next morning, when they gathered about our camp to the number of eighteen.

We were surprised to find them of diminutive stature, the tallest not exceeding three feet in height. They were excessively mischievous, and disposed to steal such trifling things as they could carry away. Their countenances are of the color of dirt, and their hair white and glossy as the silk of maize. The one that we took to be their chief was an exceedingly diminutive personage, but with a bald head which gave him a very venerable appearance. He was dressed in a dingy robe of jaconet, and was borne in the arms of one of his followers. On making them a speech, proposing a treaty, and assuring them of the protection of their great Father, Pierce, the chief was affected to tears, and on being comforted by his followers, repeatedly exclaimed, "da, da, a da, da;" which, we were informed by the interpreter, meant "father," and was intended as a respectful allusion to the President. We presented him afterwards with some beads, hawk-bells and other presents, which he immediately thrust into his mouth, saying "Goo," and crowing like a cock; which was rendered by the interpreter into an expression of high satisfaction. Having made presents to all his followers, they at length left us very well pleased, and we shortly after took up our line of march. From the notes of Dr. Bigguns I transcribe the following description of one of this deeply interesting people:

"Kearny Street native; name, Bill; height, two feet nine inches; hair, white; complexion, dirt color; eyes, blue; no front teeth; opal at extremity of nose; dress, a basquine of bluish bombazine with two gussets, ornamented down the front with crochet work of molasses candy, three buttons on one side and eight button holes on the other — leggings of tow-cloth, fringed at the bottoms and permitting free ventilation behind —one shoe and one boot; occupation, erecting small pyramids of dirt and water; when asked what they were, replied 'pies,' (word in Spanish meaning feet; suppose they might be the feet or foundation of some barbarian structure); religious belief, obscure; when asked who made him, replied 'PAR,' (supposed to be the name of one of their principal Deities)."

We broke up our encampment and moved North by compass across Market Street on the morning of the 6th, and about noon had completed the survey as far as the corner of Second Street.

While crossing Market Street, being anxious to know the exact time, I concluded to determine it by observation. Having removed the Sidereal Clock from the cart and put it in the street, we placed the cart in the plane of the Meridian and I removed the eye and object-glass of the transit, for the purpose of wiping them. While busily engaged in this manner, an individual whom I have reason to believe is connected with a fire company, approached, and seeing the large brazen tube of the transit pointed to the sky, mistook it for a huge speaking trumpet. Misled by this delusion, he mounted the cart, and in an awful tone of voice shouted through the transit, "Wash her, Thirteen!" but having miscalculated the strength of his lungs, he was seized with a violent fit of coughing, and before he could be removed had completely coughed the vertical hairs out of the instrument. I was in despair at this sudden destruction of the utility of our most valuable instrument, but fortunately recollecting a gridiron that we had among our kitchen apparatus, I directed Dr. Heavysterne to hold it up in the plane of the true Meridian, and with an opera glass watched and noted by the clock the passage of the sun's centre across the five bars. Having made these observations, I requested the principal computer to work them out, as I wished to ascertain the time immediately; but he replying that it would take some three months to do it, I concluded not to wait, but sent a man into the grocery, corner of Market and Second, to inquire the time, who soon returned with the desired information. It may be thought singular that with so many gold watches in our party we should ever be found at a loss to ascertain the time; but the fact was that I had directed every one of our employees to set his watch by Greenwich mean time, which, though excellent to give one the longitude, is for ordinary purposes the meanest time that can be found. A distressing casualty that befell Dr. Bigguns on this occasion may be found worthy of record. An omnibus, passing during the time of observation, was driven carelessly near our Sidereal Clock, with which it almost came in contact. Dr. Bigguns with a slight smile remarked that "the clock *was nearly run down,*" and immediately fainted away. The pursuits of science cannot be delayed by accidents of this nature; two of the workmen removed our unfortunate friend, at once, to the Orphan Asylum where, having rung the bell, they left him on the steps and departed, and we never saw him afterwards.

From the corner of Market to the corner of Second and Folsom Streets, the route presents no object of interest worthy of mention. We were forced to the conclusion, however, that little throwing of stones prevails near the latter point, as the inhabitants mostly live in glass houses. On the 8th we had brought the survey nearly up to Southwick's Pass on Folsom Street, and we commenced going through the Pass on the morning of the 9th. This pass consists of a rectangular ravine, about 10 feet in length, the sides lined with pine boards, with a white oak (*quercus albus*) bar that at certain occasions forms across, entirely obstructing the whole route. We found no difficulty in getting through the Pass on foot, nor with the wheelbarrows; but the mule carts and the two Fannies were more troublesome, and we were finally unable to get them through without a considerable pecuniary disbursement, amounting in all to one dollar and fifty cents ($1.50). We understand that the City of San Francisco is desirous of effecting a safe and free passage through this celebrated cañon, but a large appropriation ($220,000) is required for the purpose.

The following passages relating to this portion of the route, transcribed from the Geological Notes of Dr. Dunshunner, though not directly connected with the objects of the survey, are extremely curious in a scientific point of view, and may be of interest to the general reader.

"The country in the vicinity of the route after leaving Southwick's Pass is very productive, and I observed with astonishment that red-headed children appear to grow spontaneously. A building was pointed out to me near our line of march as the locale of a most astounding agricultural and architectural phenomenon, which illustrates the extreme fertility of the soil in a remarkable degree. A small pine wardrobe which had been left standing by the side of the house (a frame cottage with a piazza) at the commencement of the rainy season, took root and in a few weeks grew to the prodigious height of thirty feet, and still preserving its proportions and characteristic appearance, extended in each direction until it covered a space of ground some forty by twenty feet in measurement.

"This singular phenomenon was taken advantage of by the proprietors; doors and windows were cut in the wardrobe, a chimney erected, and it now answers every purpose of an addition to the original cottage, being two stories in height! This doubtless appears almost incredible, but fortunately the house and attached wardrobe may be seen any day from the road, at a trifling expense of omnibus hire, by the sceptical. Some distance beyond rises a noble structure built entirely of cut-wood, called 'The Valley House, by Mrs. Hubbard.' Not imagining that a venial species of profanity was conveyed by this legend, I concluded that Mrs. Hubbard was simply the proprietor. This brought to my mind the beautiful lines of a primitive poet, Spenser, * if I mistake not:

> Old Mother Hubbard went to the cupboard
> To get her poor dog a bone;
> But when she got there, the cupboard was bare,
> And so the poor dog got none.

"Feeling curious to ascertain if this were by any possibility the ancient residence of the heroine of these lines, perchance an ancestress of the present proprietor, I ventured to call and inquire; and my antiquarian zeal was rewarded by the information that such was the case; and that if I returned at a later hour during the evening I could be allowed a sight of the closet and a view of the skeleton of the original dog. Delighted with my success, I returned accordingly and finding the door closed, ventured to knock; when a sudden shower of rain fell, lasting but about five seconds, but drenching me to the skin. Undeterred by this contretemps, I elevated my umbrella and knocked again, loudly, when a violent concussion upon the umbrella, accompanied by a thrill down the handle which caused me to seat myself precipitately in a bucket by the side of the door, convinced me that electrical phenomena of an unusual character were prevalent, and decided me to return with all speed to our encampment. Here I was astounded by discovering inverted on the summit of my umbrella a curious and deeply interesting vase of singularly antique shape, and composed, apparently, of white porcelain. Whether this vase fell from the moon, a comet, or a passing

---

* The Doctor is in error; the lines quoted are from Chaucer. — J.P.

meteor, I have not yet decided; drawings of it are being prepared, and the whole subject will receive my thorough investigation at an early day. *

"I subsequently attempted to pursue my investigations at the 'Valley House,' but the curt manner of the proprietor led me to suspect that the subject was distasteful, and I was reluctantly compelled to abandon it.

"Near the 'Valley House' I observed an advertisement of 'The Mountain View,' by P. Buckley; but the building in which it is exhibited being closed, I had no opportunity to judge of the merits of the painting, or the skill of Mr. Buckley as an artist. A short distance further, I discovered a small house occupied by a gentleman, who appeared engaged in some description of traffic with the emigrants; and on watching his motions intently, my surprise was great to find that his employment consisted in selling them small pieces of pasteboard at fifty cents apiece! Curious to know the nature of these valuable bits of paper, I watched carefully the proprietor's motions through a window for some hours; but being at length observed by him, I was requested to leave, and I left. This curious subject is therefore, I regret to say, enwrapped in mystery, and I reluctantly leave it for the elucidation of some future savant. The beautiful idea originated by Col. Benton, that buffaloes and other wild animals are the pioneer engineers, and that subsequent explorations can discover no better roads than those selected by them, would appear to apply admirably to the Central Route. Many pigs, singly and in droves, met and passed me continually; and as the pig is unquestionably a more sagacious animal than the buffalo, their preference for this route is a most significant fact. I was, moreover, informed by the emigrants that this route was 'the one followed by Col. Fremont when he lost his men.' This statement must be received cum grano salis, as on my inquiry — 'What men?' my informant replied

---

* This curious antique, to which I have given the name of the "Dunshunner Vase," has singularly the appearance of a *wash basin*! When the drawings are completed, it is to be presented to the California Academy of Natural Sciences. — J.P.

'A box of chessmen,' which answer, from its levity, threw an air of doubt over the whole piece of information, in my mind. There can be no question, however, that Lieut. Beale has frequently travelled this route, and that it was a favorite with him; indeed, I am informed that he took the first omnibus over it that ever left San Francisco for the Mission of Dolores.

"The climate in these latitudes is mild; snow appears to be unknown, and we saw but little ice; what there was being sold at twenty-five cents per lb.

"The geological formation of the country is not volcanic. I saw but one small specimen of trap during the march, which I observed at the 'Valley House,' with a mouse in it. From the vast accumulations of sand in these regions, I am led to adopt the opinions of the ethnologists of the 'California Academy of Natural Sciences,' and conclude that the original name of this territory was Sand Francisco, from which the final 'd' in the prefix has been lost by time, like the art of painting on glass.

"Considering the innumerable villages of pigs to be found located on the line of march, and the consequent effect produced on the atmosphere, I would respectfully suggest to the Chief Engineer the propriety of changing the name of the route by a slight alteration in the orthography, giving it the appropriate and euphonious title of the 'Scentral R. R. Route.'

"Respectfully submitted,
"Abraham Dunshunner, LL.D.
"P.G.C.R.R.R.S."

From Southwick's Pass the survey was continued with unabated ardor until the evening of the 10th instant, when we had arrived opposite Mrs. Freemans's "American Eagle," where we encamped. From this point a botanical party under Prof. Weegates was sent over the hills to the S. and W. for exploration. They returned on the 11th, bringing a box of sardines, a tin can of preserved whortleberries, and a bottle of whisky, as specimens of the products of the country over which they had passed. They reported discovering on the old plank road an inn or hostel kept by a native American Irishman, whose sign exhibited the Harp of Ireland encircling the shield of the United States, with the mottoes:

ERIN GO UNUM,

E PLURIBUS BRAGH.

On the 14th the party arrived in good health and excellent spirits at the "Nightingale," Mission of Dolores.

History informs us that

> *The Nightingale club at the village was held,*
> *at the sign of the Cabbage and Shears.*

It is interesting to the Antiquarian to look over the excellent cabbage garden still extant immediately opposite the Nightingale, and much more so to converse with Mr. Shears, the respected and urbane proprietor.

The survey and *reconnoissance* being finished on our arrival at the Mission, it may be expected that I should here give a full and impartial statement as to the merits or demerits of the route, in connection with the proposed Railroad.

Some three months must elapse, however, before this can be done, as the triangulation has yet to be perfectly computed, the sub-reports examined and compiled, the observations worked out, and the maps and drawings executed. Besides, I have received a letter from certain parties interested in the Southern and Northern routes, informing me that if I suspend my opinion on the "Great Central" for the present it will be greatly to my interest — and as my interest is certainly my principal consideration, I shall undoubtedly comply with their request unless, indeed, greater inducement is offered to the contrary.

Meanwhile I can assure the public *that a great deal may certainly be said in favor of the Central Route.* A full report accompanied by maps, charts, sub-reports, diagrams, calculations, tables and statistics, may shortly be expected.

Profiles of Prof. Heavysterne, Dr. Dunshunner and my self, executed in black court plaster by Mr. Jinkins, R. A., one of the Artists of the Expedition, in his unrivalled style of elegance, may be seen for a short time at Messrs. LeCount & Strong's — scale 1 1/2 inch to one foot.

In conclusion I beg leave to return my thanks to the Professors, Assistants, and Artists of the Expedition, for the energy, fidelity and zeal with which they have ever co-operated with me and seconded my efforts; and to assure them that I shall be happy at any time to sit for my portrait for them, or to accept the handsome service of plate which I am told they have prepared for me, but feel too much delicacy to speak to me about.

I remain, with the highest respect and esteem for myself and every body else,

John Phoenix, A. M.,
Chief Engineer and Astronomer, S.F.A.M.D.C.R.

The Annexed sketch of our route, prepared by Mr. Jinkins and Kraut, is respectfully submitted to the Public. It is not, of course, compiled with that accuracy which will characterize our final maps, but for the ordinary purposes of travel will be found sufficiently correct.

J.P., A.M.C.E. & C.A.

RECONNOISSANCE
OF THE
CENTRAL RAILROAD ROUTE,
FROM
SAN FRANCISCO TO THE MISSION OF DOLORES,
By Prof. John Phœnix, Esq., A. M. & C. A. & C. E.
DRAWN BY KRAUT AND JINKINS, R. A., ARTISTS TO THE EXPEDITION.

KEARNY STREET.   (Plaza.)
1   7   8   3   4   6   7   5   1
Orphans.
NOTE—The soundings are in fathoms, showing the depth of mud and water during the rainy season.

MARKET STREET.   (a)

(a) Represents a man walking down the street at the time of the passage of the Expedition.

SECOND STREET.
Glass House.

FOLSOM (a) STREET.   Nightingale.

(a) Southwick's Pass.

E. Halfred Jinkins, Del.   *A. Kraut, Sculp.*

Letter to Secretary of War Jefferson Davis

Benicia Cal. 15 June 1855.

Hon. Jefferson Davis.
Secretary of War.

    Sir,

        I have served in California since the 1st of June 1849, with the exception of an interval of eight months. I have never applied for a leave of absence, and have always been ready to execute any duty assigned me with cheerfulness. My family reside in Massachusetts, my only surviving parent is getting old, and she begins to fear that she will never have an opportunity to see me again. If any changes should be made in the stations of officers of my Corps, and you should find it consistent with the interests of the service to order me to the East; to West Point, or to any station on the Atlantic Sea Board, you would confer on me a very great favor by doing so.

        I remain. Sir
        with high respect
        Your obt Sevt
        Geo. H. Derby
        Lieut Topl Engineers.

PHOENIX AT BENICIA

First printed in the Pioneer,
July, 1855

BENICIA, CAL., **10th June, 1855**. I observed your pathetic inquiry as to my whereabouts. I'm all right, sir. I have been vegetating for two or three weeks in this sweet (scented) place, enjoying myself after a manner in "a tranquil cot, in a pleasant spot, with a distant view of the changing sea." Howbeit, Benicia is not a Paradise. Indeed, I am inclined to think that had Adam and Eve been originally placed here, the human race would never have been propagated. It is my impression that the heat and the wind and some other little Benician accidents would have been too much for them. It would have puzzled them, moreover, to disobey their instructions; for there is no Tree of Knowledge, or any other kind in Benicia; but if they had managed this, what, in the absence of fig-leaves, would they have done for clothing? Maybe tule would have answered the purpose — there's plenty of that. I remarked to my old friend Miss Wiggins the other day in a conversation on Benicia, its advantages and its drawbacks, that there was not much society here.

"Wal," replied the old lady, "thar's *two*, the Methodists and Mr. Woodbridge's, but I don't belong to nuther."

"I don't either," said I, and the conversation terminated.

I hardly know what to write to you; I remind myself of the old Methodist Elder, way down on the French Broad in Tennessee, who was unexpectedly called upon to address a Camp-Meeting. He slowly rose and ejaculated, "Brutherin," — here an idea struck him — "Brutherin," said he, "the term *Brutherin* arose from an old custom of the Apostles, who used to go up to the tabernacle and *breathe therein!* Hence the term, Brutherin. But my brutherin," he went on, "I'm not going to take my text from any particular part of the Bible tonight. I'll tell you," said he with a pleasant smile as he warmed to his work, "I'll tell you all about old brother Paul, who went down to Corinth and got into an all-fired scrape — and was knocked down — and drug out— and left thar for dead — all of which is written by Hellicarnassus, up the Archi*pe*lago — bless-ed be the Lord!" Now, like this "ancient worthy," who by the way went on and made a very effective speech of it, I'm not going to take my text from anything in particular, but I will commence this rambling epistle by an anecdote of "old Brother" Tushmaker, which I think extremely probable had never yet been published.

Dr. Tushmaker was never regularly bred as a physician or surgeon, but he possessed naturally a strong mechanical genius and a fine appetite; and finding his teeth of great service in gratifying the latter propensity, he concluded that he could do more good in the world and create more real happiness therein by putting the teeth of its inhabitants in good order, than in any other way; so Tushmaker became a dentist. He was the man that first invented the method of placing small cog-wheels in the back teeth for the more perfect mastication of food, and he claimed to be the original discoverer of that method of filling cavities with a kind of putty, which, becoming hard directly, causes the tooth to ache so grieviously that it has to be pulled, thereby giving the dentist two successive fees for the same job. Tushmaker was one day seated in his office, in the city of Boston, Massachusetts, when a stout old fellow named Byles presented himself to have a back tooth drawn. The dentist seated his patient in the chair of torture, and opening his mouth, discovered there an enormous tooth on the right-hand side, about as large, as he afterwards expressed it, "as a small Polyglot Bible." I shall have trouble with this tooth, thought Tushmaker, but he clapped on his heaviest forceps and pulled. It didn't come. Then he tried the turn-screw, exerting his utmost strength, but the tooth wouldn't stir.

"Go away from here," said Tushmaker to Byles, "and return in a week, and I'll draw that tooth for you or know the reason why."

Byles got up, clapped a handkerchief to his jaw, and put forth. Then the dentist went to work, and in three days he invented an instrument which he was confident would pull any thing. It was a combination of the lever, pulley, wheel and axle, inclined plane, wedge and screw. The castings were made and the machine put up in the office, over an iron chair rendered perfectly stationary by iron rods going down into the foundations of the granite building. In a week old Byles returned; he was clamped into the iron chair, the forceps connected with the machine attached firmly to the tooth and Tushmaker stationing himself in the rear, took hold of a lever four feet in length. He turned it slightly. Old Byles gave a groan and lifted his right leg. Another turn; another groan, and up went the leg again.

"What do you raise your leg for?" asked the doctor.

"I can't help it," said the patient.

"Well," rejoined Tushmaker, "that tooth is bound to come now."

He turned the lever clear round, with a sudden jerk, and snapped old Byles' head clean and clear from his shoulders, leaving a space of four inches between the severed parts! They had a *post mortem* examination —the roots of the tooth were found extending down the right side, through the right leg, and turning up in two prongs under the sole of the right foot!

"No wonder," said Tushmaker, "he raised his right leg."

The jury thought so too, but they found the roots much decayed, and five surgeons swearing that mortification would have ensued in a few months, Tushmaker was cleared on a verdict of "justifiable homicide." He was a little shy of that instrument for some time afterward; but one day an old lady, feeble and flaccid, came in to have a tooth drawn, and thinking it would come out very easy, Tushmaker concluded, just by way of variety, to try the machine. He did so, and at the first turn drew the old lady's skeleton completely and entirely from her body, leaving her a mass of quivering jelly in her chair! Tushmaker took her home in a pillow-case. She lived seven years after that, and they called her the "India-Rubber Woman." She had suffered terribly with the rheumatism, but after this occurrence never had a pain in her bones. The dentist kept them in a glass case. After this, the machine was sold to the contractor of the Boston Custom-House, and it was found that a child of three years of age could, by a single turn of the screw, raise a stone weighing twenty-three tons. Smaller ones were made, on the same principle, and sold to the keepers of hotels and restaurants. They were used for boning turkeys. There is no moral to this story whatever, and it is possible that the circumstances may have become slightly exaggerated. Of course, there can be no doubt of the truth of the main incidents.

The following maritime anecdote was related to me by a small man in a pea-jacket and sou'-wester hat, who had salt standing in crusts all over his face. When I asked him if it were true, he replied, "The jib-sheet's a rope, and the helm's a tiller." I guess it's all right.

Many years ago, on a stormy and inclement evening, "in the bleak December," old Miss Tarbox, accompanied by her niece, Mary Ann Stackpole, sailed from Holmes's Hole to Cotuit, in the topsail schooner *Two Susans*. "The rains descended, and the floods came, and the winds blew and beat upon" that schooner, and great was the tossing and pitching thereof; while Captain Blackler and his hardy crew "kept her to it," and old Miss Tarbox and her niece rolled about in their uncomfortable bunks, wishing themselves back in Holmes's Hole, or any other hole, on the dry land. The shouts of Captain Blackler as he trod the deck, conveying orders for "tacking ship," were distinctly audible to the afflicted females below; and "Oh!" groaned old Miss Tarbox during a tranquil interval of her internal economy, as for the fifteenth time the schooner "went in stays," "what a drefful time them pore creeturs of sailors is a having on't. Just listen to Jim Blackler, Mary Ann, and hear how he is ordering about pore fellow *Hardy Lee*. I've heerd that creetur hollered for twenty times this blessed night, if I have onst."

"Yes," replied the wretched Mary Ann as she gave a fearful retch to starboard, "but he ain't no worse off than poor *Tauplse Hall* — he seems to ketch it as bad as Hardy."

"I wonder who they be," mused old Miss Tarbox. "I knowed a Miss Hall that lived at Seekonk Pint oncet — mebbe it's her son." A tremendous sea taking the *Two Susans* on her quarter at this instant put a stop to the old lady's cogitations; but they had an awful night of it — and still above the roaring of the wind, the whistling and clasing of the shrouds, the dash of the sea, and the tramp of the sailors, was heard the voice of stout Captain Blackler as he shouted, "Stations! *Hard a lee! Tops'* le haul! Let go and haul," and the *Two Susans* went about. And, as old Miss Tarbox remarked years afterward, when she and Mary Ann had discovered their mistake and laughed thereat, "Anybody that's never been to sea won't see no pint to this story."

PHOENIXIANA

The first edition of *Phoenixiana* appeared in 1856 and sold out immediately. Although it was priced at one dollar, the book was so popular that by the end of the year the volume had gone through several editions and had been reprinted in London. With *Phoenixiana*, Derby suddenly found himself famous. Unfortunately, the volume was edited by Judson Ames, who sold the copyright to Appleton & Co. for $450.00, and Derby never saw a penny of royalties.

Yours respectfully
John P. Squeribob

San Francisco, July 15, 1855.

"THIS book is merely a collection of sundry sketches, recently published in the newspapers and magazines of California. They were received with approval, separately, and it is to be hoped they may meet with it on their appearance in a collected form. When first published, the Author supposed he had seen and heard the last of them, but circumstances entirely beyond his control have led to their republication.

The Author does not flatter himself that he had made any very great addition to the literature of the age, by this performance; but if his book turns out to be a very bad one, he will be consoled by the reflection that it is by no means the first, and probably will not be the last of that kind, that has been given to the Public. Meanwhile, this is, by the blessing of Divine Providence, and through the exertions of the Immortal Washington, a free country; and no man can be compelled to read any thing against his inclination. With unbounded respect for every body,

The Author remains,

JOHN PHOENIX"

On July 17, 1855, Derby was dispatched to the "Indian" territories of Oregon and Washington where he was to survey and construct several military roads, including a road from Fort Vancouver to "the Dalles" on the Columbia River.

But it wasn't the Indians who would try to bushwack Derby. The lieutenant's primary challenge would be the political haggling he encountered in the Northwest territory. Miners, merchants, logging interests — everyone wanted the roads to be constructed through their property. Lieutenant Derby tried to select the most logical route — and immediately ran into trouble. After a letter writing campaign to Congress, special interests would eventually pressure Congress to replace him.

Despite the dangers and the constant rain, the dark forests seemed to help his eyes, which were begining to give him trouble. In his letters to his mother he wrote : "I can state that my eyes are better; the shade and gloom of the forest certainly did them good — I see clearer and brighter today than I have for two or three years."

As he traveled up and down the coast from Washington Territory to San Francisco, Derby found time to write for the San Francisco *Herald*, edited by his friend John Nugent, to chronicle his adventures as "Amos Butterfield" in that "disgusting country north of Oregon."

VIEW OF MOUNT HOOD FROM A POINT NEAR THE OLD MISSION BELOW THE DALLS

VIEW ON THE COLUMBIA RIVER, NEAR THE DALLS

A TRIP TO OREGON

First Printed in the San Francisco Herald, October 18, 1855

On the 16th day of September I received a letter from my correspondent in Australia which convinced me that flour was about to make an unprecedented and unheard of rise. I have been nipped slightly heretofore in flour speculations; green and inviting appeared the floury paths before my mental vision, and I regret to say that I returned from their pursuit with just a shade of the greenness adhering to me, in a figurative point of view; but this time I determined to make a sure thing of it.*

The last quotations from Oregon (which land I never hear mentioned without associating it with the idea of Bartlett pears at one dollar a piece and particularly rotten inside) showed that flour might be purchased there for five dollars per barrel. "If, then," said I to Mrs. Butterfield, "I repair to Oregon, my dear, and purchase two thousand barrels of flour at five dollars per barrel, and returning to San Francisco, incontinently

---

* Editor's Note — According to family records, Derby supplemented his meagre army salary by shipping pigs to Oregon. Derby's partner in this scheme was another young lieutenant named Ulysses S. Grant, who in 1855 was the 4th Infantry's Regimental Quartermaster in Benicia.

sell the same at eleven dollars per ditto, our circumstances will be slightly improved."

Mrs. Butterfield had seen at Guerin's a perfect love of a velvet mantle; a brown velvet mantle profusely embroidered, for which they asked but one hundred and twenty-five dollars, and she said she thought "it would be a good thing." And so I went down to the steamship *Columbia*, and purchased A stateroom, and had my trunk "dragged into camp" in stateroom "A." I detest and despise going to sea; it makes me sick at my stomach and I cannot agree with that young man who, on being reminded that "a rolling stone gathers no moss," replied, "never mind the moss — *let us roll.*" I do not like to roll at all, and I sincerely believe that the man who first invented going to sea was some most abandoned rascal, who could not under any circumstances be permitted to live on shore, and I wish from my heart he had been drowned, and the invention lost with him. So that when I had paid sixty dollars to purser Meade, who like the beverage that bears his name, is of a mild though sparkling disposition, and is moreover constantly effervescing with good humor, I went below, and gazing with a discontented air at stateroom "A," thought to myself I had given a very high price for an emetic. However, when one has made up his mind to be slain, it is certainly the best plan to employ a regular physician and have it done *secundum artem*, and it was a great relief to my mind to find the *Columbia* a clean and comfortable steamship, where if one had to die, he could at least die with decency. The Captain too had such a cheery good natured smile on his handsome face, such a roguish twinkle about his eye, such a strong expression of wishing to make every one happy about him that it was difficult to conceive that anything very disagreeable could happen where he commanded.

You must have heard of the "Dalls of the Columbia." Well, that may appear a slight digression, but the Captain is "one of them." The *Columbia* went to sea and I went to bed in the second berth in stateroom "A." As Lever's hero, Charles O'Malley, invariably remarks, after getting a lick on the back of the head, "I knew nothing more" until the arrival at Mendocino Mills. Confused visions of Mrs. Butterfield, nursing a fifty lb. sack of flour, which changed occasionally into a bowl of gruel, and then into a large wash basin, prevailed in my mind, I remember, during this period; but at Mendocino Mills I arose, girded up my loins, and the *Columbia* being very quiet, came forth like a young giant refreshed with new wine. In fact, as the Captain pleasantly remarked, I "open like a psalm book."

Then I ascertained that we had a small, though goodly company on board. There was Colonel I., going to Oregon to see if by chance his regiment, which he had vainly looked for elsewhere, might not be stationed in that Territory; and Professor D., whose genial smile gave evidence of a kindly heart, and was good for seasickness. But, above all, there was Miss Pellet — *the* Miss Pellet who delivers lectures on Temperance, Democracy, and the social virtues. I had read in some newspaper report, written by some scoffer, of Miss Pellet's lectures, wherein she was unsatisfactorily described as a "small, middle-aged female in spectacles," and was agreeably disappointed in finding her a fine looking young lady of twenty-four or five, with a very pleasant expression, sweet smile, and to all human appearance, not in the least degree strong-minded, that is, in the offensive sense of that term. That she has a kind heart and gentle disposition, one poor seasick lady, with a suffering baby — I can warmly and truly testify —and her kind and sisterly attention will be ever gratefully remembered. She was on her way to Portland, where she intended delivering some lectures, and then contemplated making a tour by land from Oregon to California. Success attend Miss Pellet.

Even a tortoise draweth suddenly in his head when smote from the rear by some evil disposed urchin with a stick; so suddenly did I disappear within the shell of stateroom "A," when the Columbia left Mendocino Mills. Then an interval elapsed, and we arrived at Trinidad. This place derives its name from the Latin words *Trinis,* three, and *Dad*, father, having been originally discovered by three Catholic priests. The town consists of about thirty mules, being packed with whiskey for the mines on Trinity river. Another interval of wash basin and gruel and we anchored at Crescent City. This little place has quite an active and bustling appearance. It is the depot of the Klamath mines and appears to be very much of a business place. At the door of the principal public house, sat a forlorn, lost looking girl, who had once been beautiful; she was neatly and handsomely dressed, but there was a look of suffering about her pale and care worn face that I shall not soon forget. I was told she was the proprietor of the establishment. Poor thing.

There is some surf at Crescent City, and unless you embark cautiously you are very liable to get your trowsers wet. I never do anything cautiously. We arrived at Port Orford one night, and disembarked Lieut. Kautz and eight mules belonging to the 4th U.S. Infantry. Lieut. Kautz commands the military post at Port Orford I was told, but what the military post is, I am not informed; probably they use it to tie the mules to. Port Orford is a small place, a very small place. I heard that the *Columbia* once got up steam and left here, without casting off one of her stern lines, and accidentally towed the whole city up the coast about forty miles before the line parted, very much to the confusion of one Tichnor, who having been elected a member of the Oregon Legislature, sailed off in a small schooner to find that body, but being unsuccessful, attempted to return to Port Orford but did not get in for some time owing to that accident.

Astoria is called because one Washington Irving (who I understood was a sargent in the rifle regiment) once made an ass of himself by writing a book about it, in which he completely exhausted the subject, or in other words, tore it all to pieces. However, Astoria will yet be a great city, as in some future letter I may demonstrate to you. Ah, how delightful was the voyage of the noble Columbia up the beautiful river whose name it bears. The sea-sickness, the wash basin, the gruel, even the flour, were all forgotten, and seated on the deck, oblivious of past sorrow we gazed on the rich and varied scenery with ecstatic delight.

The trip of the Columbia was the eighty-eighth that she has made without an accident, a fact in these times certainly worth chronicling. Our pilot, the eminent Cladwell, I am informed had acquired such proficiency in the use of the sextant that on one occasion seeing two geese flying across the river, and having no gun, he brought them both down to the horizon with that instrument, and by moving the tangent screw, actually kept them there until the boat could be sent to pick them up. A merry gentleman named Trench told me this and remarked that the geese were so fat they could not be eaten. Goose meat is always very greasy eating.

Rainier on the Columbia. This place derives its name from a little circumstance that took place in 1848. Two gentlemen, arriving at this point encamped, and shortly after a little rain squall came up, which lasted two months and four days. And then set in for a long storm. One day, during a shower of unusual violence, one of the gentlemen who, by the way, had not spoken for about four months — for it rained so hard that they could not hear each other — turned over, and with the air of one who has made up his mind on the subject, remarked, "It is rainy here."

"Yes," replied the other with confidence, "It is certainly rainy here."

So they called it "Rainy here," which has gradually been vulgarized and corrupted into Rainier.

From the Columbia River we had a glorious view of Mount Hood — that magnificient peak, towering far above the clouds, its snow-capped summit, plainly visible at a distance of one-hundred miles. For seventeen thousand feet it is one glittering sheet of snow and ice. Dryer, of the Oregonian a year or two since, procured a pair of shoes, the soles thickly studded with nails, and with a long staff with spikes in the end of it in his hand, essayed to ascend that fearful acclivity. He had, I should mention, nine pounds of pork in his coat tail pocket for provisions. Having reached an altitude of 13,480 feet, he thought he heard a noise behind him, and incautiously looking over his shoulder, up went his heels, and down came Dryer; with the velocity of the forked lightning he sped down that sheet of greased ice, making the entire descent in four and three-tenth seconds, and finally came into Portland a scratched and used up man. When he started on the ascent he had as good a black-swallow coat as you would wish to see; when he reached the bottom, the coat had become a short jacket — it never reached the bottom as a coat — and the pantaloons — well, on a clear day, with a good glass, from Vancouver, you can see very plainly on the side of the mountain the black streak that Dryer made when he slid down. He has despised mountain scenery and bushes ever since. I like to be considered a truthful person, so if any one will inform me just how much of this story they believe, I will be happy to take the rest of it back.

Portland is the largest city in Oregon; it contains 2,000 inhabitants, is situated on the Willamette River, and is called Portland because it is not a sea port. As the Columbia rounded to at the dock, every white male inhabitant of the City of Portland rushed down to meet her. She fired her gun, and every white male inhabitant shut his eyes and stooped down to dodge the wad. The arrival of the steamer is one of the great events in the lives of the people of Portland. It is supposed by Dr. Evans, the State or Territorial Geologist, (who found little latitude and longitude of the Oregon base line one day when he was out prospecting that they don't get much to eat except on these occasions, and gorging themselves to repletion when they have the opportunity, they relax into a state of supineness like amiable boa constrictors, in which they remain until the steamer comes again.

Imagine the feelings that animated my mind as we arrived — I sprang hastily from the steamer; I saw my friend Mr. Leonard & Green, the great Portland jobber and importer, on the dock. I seized him by the arm and led him to one side — "Butterfield," said he, "how do you do?"

"Never mind"" replied I, in a faltering voice; "I want to buy two thousand barrels of Oregon flour!"

Leonard & Green smiled; he was not at all excited, and he answered "Probably!" I gasped for breath. "Tell me," said I, "how is flour selling?"

Leonard & Green looked me calmly in the eye and answered slowly "Eleven dollars and a half a barrel!"

I am not a profane man; I attend the Rev. Dr. Scott's church regularly, have family prayers in my household, and say grace over my frugal repasts; but dog gorn — never mind, as the man said, "I couldn't begin to do justice to the subject."

I wrote a letter, a doleful letter to Mrs. Butterfield that night, and the brown velvet embroidered mantle still hangs in Guerin's window. I walked up the street of Portland and heard a man scream out, "J. Neely Johnston is Governor of California, ho! ho! ho!"

Confound Portland and Oregon Territory; I wish from the very bottom of my heart that Pierce would appoint John Bigler Governor of it. Yours in deep disgust,

AMOS BUTTERFIELD

Flour & Pork

NEAR THE CORNER OF BATTERY AND FRONT

Orders from the country promptly filled

"MENDOCINO"

Another kindred spirit of early California humor was Alonzo Delano (1806-1874), a writer affectionately known to his audiences as "the Old Block." The following newspaper fragment, probably authored by Delano, was originally included in the gallies of The Squibob Papers (1865) and describes a brief encounter at sea with "the Veritable Squibob."

Passing Point del Rey, we were fully at sea, going it toe- and heel over the heavy swells; and while several uneasy mortals, having paid their fare at the Captain's office, were casting up their accounts and settling some small balances with their stomachs over the rail — a sort of tribute to Old Neptune — I sat quietly alone on the quarter-deck, munching a cracker and a piece of cheese by way of lunch, having previously taken a receipt in full for all sea dues from Mr. Tompkins, before I left home. Directly, Capt. Dall approached with a gentleman, saying — "Old Block, I have the pleasure of introducing sir, John Phoenix."

My under-jaw dropped half-way in its course through the soda biscuit; my thumb and finger squeesed the cheese into fragments; I felt the warm blood (what was left in me) rushing to my face, and a thrill of pleasure shot through my whole frame, which for a moment gave me more life and animation than three doses of cod liver oil would have done, taken at once and with a full allowance of brandy in each. Squibob was before me! Resurrected in Phoenix, the Immortal Professor of Natural and Unnatural Sciences, the author, subauthor, soldier, engineer, scholar and gentleman, was before me! It was the first time we had met, although friendly espistles had passed between us many months ago. Hand in hand we sat down together, like old acquaintances, and whatever there is formal in etiquette was not thought of there; and, though I was weak, and sick, and stupid for a time, I forgot it all in the frank, hearty and kind manner of the greatest wit of California.

"He was all my fancy painted him," and I know well my friend that you don't believe a voyage can be made with him in Oregon without amusement and pleasure. Nor can it, for if you are too puritanical to like his wit, you will yield to his courtesy and kindness of heart. Scanning my countenance a moment, he said in a tone as if convinced of the fact, "Why you have got a pretty big nose."

I pardoned his optical delusion on the spot, on the ground that the refraction of the rays of light frequently produce extraordinary phenomena of optics — and furthermore, after having followed my nose for nearly fifty years, I know it is a very good nose — it has thus far answered my purpose well, and though I own it had led me into some scrapes, it has invariably led me out. Let it blow ever so hard, my nose never was wrung from its duty, upon, unless I have a cold in my head. But instead of going to Oregon, I find I've got into a chapter on noses, and there is no such promontory on the whole coast. If there is, it wasn't laid down on our charts.

If I am eating lunch in the mountains, and a miner comes along, invariably offer him a share — it is our mountain custom. So, as we were on a mountain country — for about that time "Hail Columbia" was mounting some big seas — I broke my biscuit in two and offered him half, with a share of my crushed cheese; which after looking at my gaunt and Quixotic visage, he declined, thinking probably, I needed it more than he.

We were passing Cape Mendocino, a high bluff promontory; standing isolated from the shore, a little distance in the sea, was a huge mass of rock, unevenly rounded off, based apparently on a platform which partly surrounded it. An irregular archway showed a deep excavation, a cave which appeared to be capacious, extending far into the rock, as if it was the grand entrance to some giant's castle. It was guarded by scores of sea dogs, which, as we passed, began to move their heads from side to side in a most clumsy manner, and dragging their unwieldy forms to the edge of the platform they dashed with a heavy splash into the sea, as our own puffing monster neared them, much to the amusement of the passengers. A knot of gentlemen stood gazing from the deck at the curious rock and the bold bluff in the background, when someone inquired what the promontory derived its curious name from. Phoenix being a universal Encyclopedia, gave a clear and livid exposition of its origin:

"In former times," he said, "it was a fishing station; occasionally the fisherman would break their nets and start for their quarters in the castellated rock. As they were going in, other parties would inquire the cause of their going ashore, calling loudly after their comrades, "What are you going ashore for?" To which they replied, "To mend a seine, O!" which has been perverted by vulgar translation to "Mend-o-cino." There was no disputing the text, and the explanation was deemed perfectly satisfactory.

BUTTERFIELD AT THE BALL

First Printed in the San Francisco Herald, December 31, 1855

You have not heard from me for some time. I have been "round," however, which is a pleasant metaphorical way of expressing the fact that I have been about, and is not intended as an allusion to my figure, though I weigh two hundred and forty-three net, and it might appear appropriate to scoffers. Since my unfortunate expedition to Oregon, I have been attending closely to my legitimate business, and do not mind saying that I have been tolerably successful. I did a little thing in butter last week, not after the manner of the celebrated sculptor Canova — who, I am told, used to carve horses and other animals out of that oleaginous substance, which looked well but became unpleasant to the smell in a short time — but in the way of speculation, which increased my satisfaction and my balance at Doolittle, Walker & Leggett's, my bankers, in no small degree.

I was sitting in my counting-room a few days since, in an amiable frame of mind, thinking of that butter which I had sold to a manufacturer to grease the wheels of his manufactory, and wondering whether its strength increased the power of the machinery, when Podgers, of Gawk & Podgers, Battery Street, dropped in.

"Butterfield," said he, "don't you want to go to a ball?"

A vision of Mrs. Butterfield resplendent in her new dress, which, though of late importation, she calls "*more antique,*" passed before my mind. I thought of the balance at Doolittle's, and in my usual prompt and decided manner replied, "Well, I don't know."

"It's a complimentary ball," said Podgers, "given for the benefit of the officers of the Army and Navy, and comes off at Madame Pike's on Friday." (The name is Pique, and is pronounced *Pi-quee*, but Podgers don't understand French.)

Now I always liked the officers, poor fellows; they look so pretty in their brass-mounted clothes, and walk around with such a melancholy air, as though they were wondering how they manage to support existence on their pay and allowance — and how the deuce they do puzzles me. So after a few words more with Podgers, we started off to purchase the necessary pasteboard. I suppose it was because the ball was a national affair that we went to the United States Mint for that purpose. Here we were introduced to a singularly handsome young fellow, who gazed rather dubiously on Podgers and myself when he preferred our request.

"The ball is to be very select," said he.

"Ah," replied I, "that's exactly the reason we wish to patronize it."

The young gentleman could not withstand the smile with which these words were accompanied.

"What name?" said he.

"Butterfield," I replied.

"Flour and Pork," said he, with a kindly expression.

"Corner of Battery and Front," I answered, and the thing was done. Podgers got his ticket also, and we left the Mint arm in arm, wondering if the lovely design for a head on the new three dollar piece was intended for a likeness of the U.S. Treasurer, of whose agreeable countenance we caught a glimpse as we retired. Mrs. Butterfield was delighted, so was Austin, I fancy; he sent me a note a day or two after, very prettily conceived, with Honiton, Valenciennes, point, edging, and other hard words in it, which must have given him great satisfaction to compose. I purchased of Keyes (not that Keyes, but the other firm a new blue dress coat with brazen buttons, military, you know; a pair of cinnamon colored leg scabbards, and a very tasty thing in the way of a vest, garnet colored velvet with green plush cross bars, in which I fancied I should create something of a sensation. I also dropped in at Tucker's, and seeing a pretty breastpin in the form of a figure 2, which he said was a tasteful conceit for married men, showing that there were two in the family, I bought that also, and hereby acknowledge that it has given me great satisfaction. Friday evening at last arrived. Podgers was to come for us in a carriage at 8 o'clock, and we commenced dressing at three, immediately after dinner. My friends have sometimes flattered me by remarking something in my air and personal appearance resembling the late Daniel Webster (formerly Secretary of State under Tyler's administration). After dressing, and going through the operation which Mrs. Butterfield unpleasantly terms prinking, I walked into the room of our next neighbor (we board at the corner of Stockton and Powell), under the pretense of borrowing a candle. He was sitting by the fire smoking a cigar and reading Tennyson's poems, which I take this opportunity of declaring are the silliest trash I ever had the misfortune to get hold of.

"Mr. Brummell," said I complacently, "do you think I look at all like the great Daniel?" Brummell gazed on me with evident admiration.

"Yes," he replied, "but you are not near as heavy as he was."

"No?" said I, "Why Daniel Webster was not a *very* large man."

"Oh!" replied he, "I thought you alluded to Daniel Lambert."

This was a damper.

We worked for three mortal hours getting little Amos to sleep. That child is two years of age, possesses a wakefulness of disposition perfectly astonishing in one so young, and has a pleasing peculiarity of howling terrifically in the night at intervals of about twenty-five minutes. Paregoric and taffy were too much for him this time, however; he succumbed at last, and dropped peacefully to repose at half-past seven, to a second. At eight, Podgers and the carriage arrived. Mrs. Podgers came up in Mrs. Butterfield's room to show herself. She was tastefully and magnificently attired. She wore a white crape illusion with eighteen flounces, over a profusely embroidered tulle skirt, looped up on the side with a bouquet of swiss meringues. Her bodice was of sea-green tabbinet, with an elegant pincushion of orange-colored *moire antique* over the bertha. Her head-dress was composed of cut velvet cabbage leaves, with turnip *au naturel*, and a small boned turkey secured by a golden wire, "*a la maitre d'hotel*," crowned the structure. Podgers gazed upon her with complacent and pardonable pride. We descended to the carriage, but finding it impossible for all of us to ride within, Mrs. Podgers stood upon the seat with the driver, Mrs. Butterfield and I got inside, and Podgers walked. [By the way, on this account, he subsequently, in an unjustifiable manner, objected to paying his proportion of the expenses of transportation, as had been agreed upon between us.] On arriving at Mrs. Piquee's, I regret to say, an unpleasant altercation took place between myself and our driver on the subject of the fare. I was finally compelled to close the discussion by disbursing ten dollars, which that disagreeable individual unnecessarily remarked, "was only a dollar a hundred after all."

On entering the hall, which was brilliantly illuminated, we were struck with its size and elaborate ornaments, and also with the unpleasant fact that nobody was there. The fact is, we had arrived a little too early. However, we amused ourselves walking about, and Podgers got into the supper room, where he broke a sugar chicken off the top of a large cake, to carry home to his little Anna Maria, and being detected therein, was summarily ejected, and had the chicken taken away from him, at which Mrs. B. and I secretly rejoiced. At ten o'clock, the company began to arrive, and in half an hour the large hall was crowded with the beauty, fashion and extravagance of the city. It really brought tears of delight to my eyes to see the number of lovely women that San Francisco can produce, and to think what immense sums of money their beautiful dresses must cost their husbands and fathers. Sets of quadrilles were formed, then followed the fancy dances, polkas, redowas, and that funny dance where the gentleman grabs the lady about the waist with one hand, and pumps her arm up and down with the other, while hopping violently from side to side, after the manner of that early and estimable Christian — St. Vitus.

I cannot pretend to enumerate the ladies whose charms particularly impressed me. Moreover, if I could, it would be of little service to the public, for it is in the fashion to do this sort of thing by initials, and who would recognize "lovely Mrs. A., with her ugly daughter, in white cottonet, and magnificent Mrs. B., the cynosure of all eyes in a *peignoir* of three ply carpeting, with a *corsage de gunny bag* and a *point applique robe de nuit*, or the sweet Misses C. in elaborate Swiss ginghams, with gimp cord and tassels and a *fauteuil de cabriolet*."

Suffice it to say that the loveliest ladies of San Francisco were there, and the belle of the evening was unquestionably Miss ——, though many preferred the mature charms of the radiant Mrs.——. [You perceive that these blanks are left for the convenience of those who wish to send this description to the Eastern States, who hereby have my express permission to insert any names they may think appropriate.] One lady, I observed, whose dress, though no great judge of dry goods, I should imagine to have cost in the neighborhood of fifty barrels of pork. Everything went off admirably. Wobbles, of Wobbles & Strycum — who was present with his daughter, a young lady of nine years, with a violent propensity to long curls, dressed in crimson silk with orange colored pantalettes — Wobbles, who has a very pretty way of saying poetical things, remarked with great originality that "soft eyes spoke love to eyes that spoke again, and all went berry as a marriage mell," and I agreed with him.

The officers were all there, moreover, radiant in brass coats and blue buttons — I mean blue buttons and brass coats — and looking divinely. One of them accidentally trod on my toe, but before I could utter the exclamation of anguish that I was about to give vent to, he said so sweetly "Don't apologise," that the pain left me in a moment. The officers of the *Vincennes*, though sufficiently handsome, are not tall men. This, Podgers remarked, was a dispensation of Divine Providence, as the *Vincennes* is only four feet six between the decks, and they would be constantly bumping their heads if they were taller.

At two o'clock we sat down to supper. Magnificent indeed — turkeys, chickens, salads, champagne — everybody gobbling and guzzling everything, presenting to my mind a far finer spectacle than the vaunted Falls of Niagara, which I think have been much overrated.

Podgers, who is always doing something unpleasant, emptied a plate of oyster soup on my head, merely saying, "Beg pardon, Butterfield," in consequence of which I found a large stewed oyster in my right whisker on returning to the ball room, and was made exceedingly uncomfortable during the rest of the morning.

The ball was delightful. I heard the Consul of New Zealand say it was *ravissant*, and though with but a dim idea of his meaning, I am sure it was. We returned home at 3 1/2 A.M. The street around our residence was lighted up as if for a celebration; people stood around the doorsteps, and an old gentleman with a watchman's rattle in his hand, both slightly sprung, was leaning out of an upper window of No. 3 below. A loud shout hailed us as we approached, but high above that shout, loud above the whirr of the rattle, shrill above the rolling of our carriage, sounded an alarum that we recognized but too well. It was the voice of our little Amos.

The dear child had woke up the whole street, and it is a marvel that he had not awakened the sleepers in John Jones of Peter's cemetery, "just beyond." The name of Butterfield, as you well know, is synonymous with that of Truth — but if that boy hadn't shattered every pane of glass in our front windows, and loosened all the top bricks of the chimney by the concussion of the air produced by his screaming, I wish I may never sell another lot of extra clear bacon. The paper was loosened from the walls, the plaster falling from the ceiling, the wash basin and — everything was broken, and there lay Amos black in the face, gurgling in his throat, and his small blue legs kicking up toward Heaven. We did not get asleep until rather late that morning — and what with damages, repairs, hack drivers, dresses and tickets. — the little balance at Doolittle, Walker & Leggett's is nearly exhausted.

Perhaps we shall go to another ball at Madame Pique's, soon, if so, I will send you an account of it.

Very Truly yours,

AMOS BUTTERFIELD

Flour & Pork

NEAR THE CORNER OF BATTERY AND FRONT

Country orders solicited and promptly filled, etc.

Between intervals of duty in the forests of Oregon, Derby continued to write letters to the San Francisco *Herald,* edited by his friend John Nugent. Under his pen name "John Phoenix," Derby scoffed at the "important" topics of the day — such as Jose Limantour's claim to Alcatraz, Yerba Buena, and the Farallones Islands. Derby also drew cartoons known as "The Ingenious Boy" which parodied mechanical wonders like the newly invented screwdriver. He made fun of earthquakes, spiritual mediums, and on May 4, 1856 Derby brashly burlesqued the promoters of the Oakland Bridge Project.

The idea of spanning the shallow portions of the San Francisco Bay to the wharves of San Francisco had been a dream of City Fathers since the founding of "Yerba Buena," but as an engineer, Derby knew that the technology was not available, and the dream of building one of the longest bridges in the world would not be realized until nearly 75 years later. Nevertheless, by 1855 unscrupulous promoters had seized upon the idea and were selling profitable franchises to the gullible public, and in April 1856 the proposal for building the San Francisco Bay Bridge was resusitated in the California Assembly under a bill granting right of way for a railway.

The *Herald* editorialized against the "absurdity" of building a bridge costing almost "a million dollars," and humorist Stephen Massett capitalized on the public's interest by setting to music one of Charles Mackay's poems which he entitled "The Song of the Oakland Bridge."

Derby's reply appeared in the *Herald* on May 4, 1856.

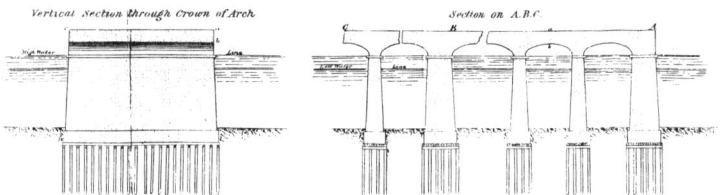

1872 Graphic, Courtesy W. Graham Arader III

SONG OF THE "OAKLAND BRIDGE"

First Printed in the San Francisco Herald, May 4, 1856

WE HAVE been favored with the perusal of the new song "O'er the Bay," or "The Song of the Oakland Bridge," the words of which are by Charles Jackey, and the music by our talented fellow-townsman, John Phoenix, Esq., and by the kindness of the latter gentleman are enabled to present our readers with the following copy, several days in advance of the Press.

O'ER THE BAY

"SONG OF THE OAKLAND BRIDGE"

Words by Charles Jackey ... Music by Pro. John Phoenix, L.L. Dr.

Dedicated to M. L. Winn, Esq., the earliest Pie-oneer of the Pacific Coast with copious explanations by the Author.

I.

The poet calls on people of energy to commence immediately the building of the Oakland Bridge, and suggests that the hydraulic characters that raise houses in such mysterious manner should assist in pumping out the Bay as a preparatory step.

Men of might be up and doing, Right away;
Drive the piles, the mud so blue in,
'Cross the Bay —
Men of suction, help 'em do it,

Descriptive of some of the usual disagreeable incidents of the passage to Oakland in the ferry-boat, on which the author once paid four bits for a passage and two bits for a bottle of execrable soda water.

YERBA BUENA ISLAND

That's the way.
There's a horse about to kick,
There's a man that's taken sick,
There's a boy that holloas Wo!
here's a nose about to blow,
There's an hourly steamboat
sticking on the way —
Men of Clinton and of Oakland —
In the Bay.

II.

The Poet pictures the families of San Francisco seeking the pleasures of rural retirement, and the wealthy merchant enjoying a drive on the completion of the bridge.

He urges the commencement of the work and calls on our richest bankers (who are hereby requested to pardon the liberty taken with their names) to assist therein.
He alludes with a sigh to pecuniary liability.

Once that welcome route is opened,
Who shall say
What happy families will move across
the Bay —
What fat old merchant there shall drive
In his chay
Drive the piles, lay the plank,
Pump the Bay dry, here's the crank;
Help us Palmer, help us Cook,
Build the bridge "by hook or crook,"
Till o' er it rattle buggy, dog-cart, dray,
(With but a trifling toll of fifty cents
to pay)
To Alameda and to Oakland,
O' er the Bay.

III.

The Poet shows the advantage of the bridge in the pursuit of fugitives from justice.

Lo! A loafer's going to vanish
Some fine day,
With a carpet-bag he's bolter,
making way;

Song of the Oakland Bridge

"In the door," — this expression is from "Hearn's History of Monte"" — it implies that he has him securely.

A beautiful picture is here presented — the Sheriff returning in luxurious ease with his prisoner, while the honest fishermen earn their living by leaning o'er the railing of the Bridge and catching the fragrant "porgie."

It is a melancholy thing that such a song as this should have an end, but, alas! "sich is life."

Lo! the Sheriff puts out after,
O' er the Bay —
He pays the toll — an awful bore —
And gets the loafer "in the door;"
And o' er the bridge he brings him back,
Or peradventure takes a hack,
(For a snug sum the City had to pay,)
While fishermen catch "porgies"
in the Bay
To sell in Clinton or in Oakland,
O' er the way.

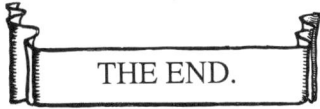

THE END.

This wonderful production, Professor Phoenix assures us, admits of a *"Choriouse"* ad libitum; which may be effected by repeating the last two lines as often as may be considered necessary, with variations to suit — the air being purposely rendered capable of the most incredible number of changes. The song may be had at LeCount's (after it is published), beautifully lithographed, and with a vignette by Nahl, giving a most touching and pathetic view of the Pile Driver, and the Steam Ferryboat, lying stuck in the mud in the distance. Price $1, or 14 copies for 50 cents.

It rained so much in Oregon, Derby wrote, that it washed off men's hair and animals acquired scales, like creatures of the deep. He had seen many funny things in Oregon, Derby continued, and would have laughed too, if his mouth hadn't filled with rain before he was half-finished.

Derby was ecstatic when his request for a transfer to the East Coast was finally granted, and on October 20, 1856 the Derbys left San Francisco by steamer. On the first of November, however, Mary gave birth prematurely to their son, forcing them to stay in Panama until Mary recovered. The child was christened George McClellan, after Derby's fellow officer from West Point, but because the child was born at sea, Derby jokingly nicknamed the boy "Pacificus."

After a brief stop in Washington, Derby secured a leave of absence from Jefferson Davis, the Secretary of War, and he returned to gloomy Boston, which was as cold as "the Island of Ichaboe." Derby's departure from the congenial environment of California, which nurtured his wit, and his return to Boston was a literary disaster. His book *Phoenixiana* was phenomenally successful in the West, yet on the East Coast Derby and his talents were ignored. Half the lieutenant's time, it seemed, was spent writing letters to the War Department concerning discrepancies in his travel vouchers or explaining his actions in the Washington Territories.

The miserable Boston winter weather bothered him, and the only person on the East Coast who seemed to care about his writing was Lewis Gaylord Clark, the editor of the *Knickerbocker.* Clark had republished many of the John Phoenix sketches and had introduced Derby to his readers as "the great Squibob all the way from California."

Derby contributed articles to *Knickerbocker* throughout 1856, parodying railway travel and staid Boston society. Characteristically, Derby even had the audacity to satirize the newly invented sewing machine, and his July, 1856 article on the "Sewing Machine Feline Attachment" produced a flood of letters to the editor.

BOSTON, A MORAL CITY

First Published Knickerbocker, February, 1857 (**SQUIBOB PAPERS**)

It is Sunday in Boston. I have been sitting in my room, No. 78 Tremont House by the window, which commands a cheerful view of a graveyard, musing on various matters and things in a solemn state of mind well befitting the place and the occasion. Seventeen inches of snow fell last night, and Boston looks white like the Island of Ichaboe, and to the full as desolate. Through the hollow and reverberating passages of this ancient building; around the corners of the sinuous streets; from each door and window, in every private and public building; and from the houses of God, resounds the peculiar sharp, hacking cough of the population of Boston. Every soul of them has it. It is the disease of the country. When I meet an acquaintance in the street, I abstain from the usual greeting, and invariably say, "How is your cough?" and the reply invariably is, "About the same."

Coughing, and the ancient pastime of hawking, (followed by expectoration) are the principal amusements in this cold city. In the graveyard beneath my window, on a slate tombstone, may be found, I am informed, the following touching inscription:

"Here I lie breft of breath,
Because a cough carried me off,
Then a coffin, they carried me off in;"

which, I doubt not, describes the case of the majority of the silent incumbents of that place of rest.

The Tremont House is in many respects a good institution; it is perfectly clean and well arranged, the attendance is good and the fodder excellent; but there is an indescribable air of gloom and solemnity pervading the entire establishment, well suited to Boston, but chilling to a stranger to the last degree. The waiters, dressed in black with white neckcloths, move silently and sadly about the tables, looking like so many Methodist ministers with thirteen children, four hundred a year, and two donation parties; the man in the office never smiles — in any point of view; a large Bible with the name of the House stamped upon it in gilt letters (to prevent religious strangers from bottling it) lies on every table, and the chambermaids attend family prayers in the basement. All is "grand, gloomy," and it must be confessed, exceedingly peculiar. I have attempted but two jokes in this solemn place, and they fell like the flakes of snow, silent and unnoticed. An unfortunate individual in the reading-room last evening was seized with an unusually violent fit of coughing, which, if a man could by any possibility be turned inside out, would have done it; and as a partial cessation of it occurred, with his hair standing on end, (he had coughed his hat off) his face glowing with exertion, and the tears standing in his unhappy eyes, he very naturally gave vent to a profane execration. Everybody looked shocked! I remarked in an audible tone to my companion that the exclamation was a coffer-dam; an admirable contrivance for raising obstructions from the bottom of streams, and probably adopted by the gentleman to clear his throat. But no one laughed, and I incontinently went to bed.

This morning on arising I discovered that my boots, left outside the door to be embellished with blacking, had, like those of Bombastes, not been displaced; so I said to the porter, a man of grave and solemn aspect:

"You have a very honest set of people about this house."

"Why?" said the porter, with a somewhat startled expression.

"Because," I rejoined, "I left my boots outside my door last night, and find this morning no one has touched them."

That man walked off all slow and stately, and never knew that I had been humorous. Disappointments have been my lot in life. I remember in early childhood going to the theatre to see Mrs. W. H. Smith appear in two pieces; the bills said she would do it, and she came on the stage perfectly whole and entire like any other lady.

Upon the whole it is my impression that Boston is a dull, gloomy, precise, and solemn city, which I take to be owing entirely to the intense cold that prevails there in the winter, which chills and freezes up to the warmer nature of the inhabitants, who don't have time to get thawed out before the cold comes back again. I have met many Bostonians in more genial climates, who appeared to be very hearty and agreeable fellows.

I took a short ride yesterday in the Metropolitan Rail-Road cars, which are dragged by horse-power from the Tremont House to Roxbury. The only other occupant of my car was a young and lovely female in deep mourning. She wore a heavy, black veil, and her thick and auburn hair was gathered up on each side her face beneath a spotless cap, a widow's cap of snowy muslin. I had always a feeling for widows; young and pretty widows particularly, always excite my deepest interest and sympathy. I gazed with moistened eye on the sweet specimen before me, so young, so beautiful, I thought, but alas! What suffering she has experienced! I pictured to myself her devotion to her husband during his last illness, the untiring watchfulness with which she hung over his pillow, the unwearying and self-sacrificing spirit with which she hoped on, hoped ever, till in despite of her care, her love, he sank forever, and her agonized shriek rang in my ear, as with hands clasped and upturned eye, she felt that he was dead, her dream of life was over, her strength was gone, her heart was broken.

The young widow had been regarding me earnestly during this time, and probably imagined what was passing in my mind, for throwing her veil over her hat, she turned partly around toward me, and looked steadfastly in my face — she winked her eye! Yes, sir, she winked her eye at *me* — the moral Phoenix; and I rose from my ashes and left the metropolitian car and returned to the Tremont House. And is it possible, thought I, as I gazed from my window up Tremont Street and observed a sanctimonious gentleman in a long black overcoat look hastily up and down the street and then dodge up a small alley in great haste; is it possible that this little widow in the car is at all typical of the great city to which she belongs? A most respectable, staid, and solemn outward appearance — covering a very strong disposition to that deviltry which is defined by the Bible as 'the lust of the flesh, the lust of the eye, and the pride of life?' But Boston, clothed in its robe of snow, looked too pure, too bride-like and I dismissed the supposition from my mind.

I had intended to have written to you more at length, but am off to New Orleans directly, and must pack my trunk. Boston is a great place. I am sorry I hadn't time to go and see the Monastery presided over by Abbot Lawrence, that was burned by the Orangemen. Yours truly and respectfully,

JOHN PHOENIX

JOURNEY FROM BOSTON
TO NEW ORLEANS

First published in Knickerbocker, April, 1857 (SQUIBOB PAPERS)

N*ew Orleans, LA.* On the fifth of January, at eight A.M., I left the Tremont House in a hackney carriage, the wheels whereof had turned into runners. This method of progression, rendered necessary by the deep snows, is considered a great amusement in the North. Being particularly dangerous to life and limb, and usually terminating in pulmonary consumption, the pastime is very properly called sleighing.

With a through-ticket for the great city of Cairo in my pocket, I took a seat in the cars at the Worcester rail-road depot. After waiting half-an-hour, during which time my sympathies were deeply interested by the performance of an unhappy young couple, one of whom was going somewhere and the other wasn't, and who in consequence were slobbering over each other to a terrible extent, a sudden harsh bark was heard from the engine, followed by a grating jar, which acted on my teeth like lemon-juice, and we were off. The motion of a rail-road car is of two kinds, which may be called the "heave and set, or whip-saw movement," and the "tip and sifter," names sufficiently expressive to require no further explanation. We started on the "heave and set," which gradually merged into the "tip and sifter" as our velocity increased.

On entering a rail-road car the first object of the solitary traveller should be to secure an entire seat to himself. This may generally be done successfully by taking the outside seat and skilfully disposing a small carpet-bag, great coat, umbrella, and cane, so as to cover the inner one. As the passengers throng into the car, many will gaze earnest at the place thus occupied, but will usually prefer to move on rather than give you trouble. But if the car is quite filled, the question will undoubtably be asked, "Is that seat taken, Sir?" when you should reply with an imperturbable countenance, "It is, Sir!" and the inquirer, with perhaps a slight glance of suspicion, will move on.

As a man's object should be to make himself as comfortable as possible in this world, that his mind may be in a proper frame to prepare for the next, a slight deviation from truth for the purpose of securing this object, like the above, is quite pardonable, in which opinion I am corroborated by my dear friend and Christian teacher, Rev. H.B.— — tch—s, whose celebrated and useful aphorism, "Never lie, unless it is necessary," will doubtless recur to the reader's mind.

Having made my arrangements in accordance with these views, and being as comfortable as circumstance would permit, the motion of the cars being that of a small boat in a high sea, and their noise like unto a steam saw-mill, I composed myself to the journey. At Framingham the usual nuisances of rail-road cars commenced. First appeared the small boy with the Boston newspapers, which had been brought to him by our train; then the dirty boy, with parched corn, who, in the intervals of trade, dabbles among his merchandise with his sore hand, and devours so much of that dry commodity that you are fain to believe him to be his own best customer; then the big boy with the fearful apples, "three for five cents;" and finally that well-known, and most indefatigable wretch with the "lozengers," who on this occasion actually sold a roll to the description called "checkerberry" to an elderly individual of the Muggins family sitting near me, who ate them, and to my great joy, became woefully disordered in consequence.

But the boy with the accordeon was not there — I think he has not yet got so far North. It was but a week before that I met him, however on the Phildelphia cars. It was after seven o'clock; the train had passed New Brunswick, and the passengers were trying to sleep (ha! ha!) when the boy entered. He was a seedy youth, with a seal-skin cap, a singularly dirty face, a gray jacket of the ventilating order, and a short but remarkably broad pair of "corduroy-corduroys." He wore an enormous bag or haversack about his neck, and bore in his hand that most infernal and detestable instrument, an accordeon. I despise that instrument of music. They pull the music out of it, and it comes forth struggling and reluctant, like a cat drawn by the tail from an ash-hole or a squirrel pulled shrieking from a hollow log with a ram-rod. This unprincipled boy commenced pulling at his thing and horrified us with the most awful version of "Dog Tray" that I ever listened to. Then he walked around the car and collected forty-two cents. Then he returned to the center of the car, and standing close to the stove, which was red hot — the night being cold — he essayed to pull out "Pop Goes the Weasel," when suddenly *pop* went the boy, he dropped the accordeon, burst into tears, and clapping his hands behind him, executed a frantic dance, accompanied by yells of the most agonizing character. I saw it all, and felt grateful to a retributive Providence. He had stood too close to the stove and his corduroys were in a light blaze; a few inches below the termination of the gray jacket was the seat of his woe. After he got on fire the conductor put him out, and a sweet and ineffable calm came over me. I realized that "whatever is, is right," and I fell into a deep and happy sleep.

The musical nuisance, fortunately was spared us on this occasion. A tourist travelling by rail-road across the United States should have but little opportunity to collect notes for his forthcoming work. Thus my idea of Albany, at which Dutch village we arrived shortly after dark, are a hasty scramble down a platform; then huddling into a sled with other bewildered and half-frozen passengers; then a rapid foot-race of about a quarter of a mile, encouraged by shouts of "Leg it! The cars are off."

"No they ain't; plenty of time."

"Hi! Hi! There round the corner, them's the cars."

Etc.; then more cars and we ground on.

It was on this Albany and Buffalo train that a little incident occurred which may be worthy of mention, and serve as a caution to future innocent travellers. I had observed that at each change of cars (and they were frequent when the general scramble took place) one car was defended from assault by a stalwart man, usually of the Irish persuasion, who deaf to menaces, unsoftened by entreaty and uncorrupted by bribes, maintained his post for the benefit of the "ledies."

"Ledies car, Sir, av ye please, forrid cars for gintlemen without leddies."

Need I say that this car so reserved was by far the most comfortable of the train, and that with that stern resolve which ever distinquishes me in the discharge of my duty for myself, I determined to get into it *coute qui coute*. So when we changed cars at Utica, I rushed forth, and seeing a nice young person with a pretty face, bonnet and shawl, and a large portmanteau, urging her way through the crowd, I stepped up by her side and with my native grace and gallantry offered my arm and my assistance. They were gratefully accepted, and proud of my success, I ushered my fair charge up to the platform of the ladies' car. My old enemy was holding the door.

"Is that your lady, Sir?" said he.

With an inward apology to Mrs. Phoenix for the great injustice done to her charms by the admission, I replied: "Yes."

Judge of my horror when this low employee of a monopolizing and unaccommodating rail-road company addressing my companion with the tone and manner of an old acquaintance, said: "Well, Sal, I guess you've done well, but I don't believe his family will think much of the match."

However, I got into the ladies' car and having repudiated the young person Sarah, got an exceedingly pleasant seat by the side of a very warm and comfortable young lady of a sleepy turn and quiet disposition. I wouldn't have changed her for two buffalo-robes, but alas! She got off at Syracuse, and then, frosty Caucasus, how cold it was! And so grinding, and jolting, jarring, sliding, and freezing, wore away the long night.

In the morning we were at Buffalo. I saw nothing of it but a rail-road depot; but I remember thinking as I stamped my feet and thrashed my arms to restore the circulation, that if that sort of weather continued "the Buffalo girls couldn't come out to-night," and would probably have to postpone their appearance until the summer season.

Among the passengers on the Erie rail-road was a very interesting family, on their way to Terre Haute, Indiana. There was the father, a fine manly figure; the mother, a pale, delicate, and lady-like; and niece, cousins, and babies innumerable, but all pretty and pleasant to behold. But the gem of the family was "Belle." Belle was the factorum, she nursed the babies, went errands for her father, helped her mother, and was always on hand to render assistance to any body, anywhere; and though her patience must have been sorely tried, she preserved her amiability and genuine good nature so thoroughly that she became to me an object of constant attention and admiration. She was evidently the manager of that family, and went about every thing with a business-like air, quite refreshing to observe. She was about sixteen years old, very pretty, neatly dressed, and of a most merry and vivacious disposition, as was evinced by every sparkle of her bright eyes. Farewell, "Belle," probably you'll never see this tribute from your unknown admirer, or meet him in *propria personae;* but the loss will hardly be felt, for you must have more admirers already than you know what to do with. Happy is the man that's destined to ring the Belle of Terre Haute.*

All day and all night we ground on, "ripping and staving." We passed through Columbus where the people had been having a grand ball to celebrate the completion of their State Capitol, and picked up three hundred and eighty-four survivors, each of whom contained a pint and a half of undiluted whiskey. And so in the morning we came to Cincinnati, where for fifteen minutes we tarried at the Burnett House, the most magnificent hotel in the United States. Here I met with Fisher, the celebrated rail-road traveler, who accompanied us to Sandoval, and with whom I was particularly charmed. Fisher is the original inventor of that ingenious plan of getting rid of an unpleasant occupant of the same seat, by opening the window on the coldest night so that the draught shall visit searchingly the back of the victim's neck; and of that method of taking up the seat and disposing it as an inclined plane, and going to sleep thereon in such a complicated manner as to defy subsequent intrusion. What he does not know about rail-roads is of no manner of consequence and useless to acquire. Thanks to his experience, we enjoyed the luxury of two seats together, and it was with deep regret that I parted with him at Sandoval.

The change of cars from the Erie to the Illinois Central is a delightful incident. The latter has the broad gauge, the seats are comfortable and convenient, the speed exhilarating, and no exertion is spared by the civil conductors to render the passengers as happy as circumstances will permit. I have never

* Editor's Note — This bawdy pun reportedly went unnoticed until publication and caused the editors great consternation.

traveled more comfortably than on the Illinois Central, and hereby wish long life and prosperity to the company.

The third day and the third night were over, we had passed safely through the city of Sandoval, which consists of one house, where the cars are detained five hours for the benefit of an aged villain who gave us very poor roasted buzzard and called it wild turkey; and, grateful to Providence, we arrived at Grand Cairo.

I stepped out of the cars a shorter man than when I started. The friction for three days and three nights had reduced my height two-and-a-half inches; a singular psychological fact, which I recommend to the consideration of the learned Walker.

Cairo is a small hole at the junction of the Ohio and the Mississippi River, surrounded by an artificial bank to prevent inundation. There are here about thirteen inhabitants, but the population is estimated at three thousand. that being a rough estimate of the number of people that were once congregated there, when five trains of cars arrived before a boat left for New Orleans. They were enjoying the luxury of the small-pox at Cairo when we arrived; they are always up to something of the kind; a continued succession of amusements followed. The small-pox having terminated its engagement, the cholera makes its appearance, and is then followed by yellow fever for the season. Sweet spot! Dickens has immortalized it under the name of Eden, an evident misnomer, for no man worth as much as Adam could remain there by any possibility.

The fine steamer *James Montgomery* was about to leave for New Orleans, and we soon found ourselves most comfortably, indeed luxuriously established on board. A very merry passage we had to this great Crescent City, under the charge of our stout and jovial captain, whose efforts to amuse us, seconded as he was by the pretty and vivacious "widow," were entirely successful. The "General" also, a noble specimen of the gentleman of Tennessee, proved himself a most agreeable traveling companion, and endeared himself to our little society by his urbanity, cheerfulness and fund of amusing and interesting anecdotes. Among our passengers was, moreover, the celebrated Eliza Logan, probably the finest actress now on the American stage, who has acquired a most enviable popularity, not only by her great professional talent, but by her charms of conversation and her estimable reputation as a lady. She chants the "Marseillaise" in a style that would delight its author. One who wishes to realize for an instant what death is, should listen to her enunciation of the last words of the refrain of this celebrated composition; if he can repress a shudder, he is something more or less than man.

Accompanied by my old friend Butterfield, who had joined us at Memphis, I landed at New Orleans, and proceeded forthwith to the Saint Charles Hotel. At this great tavern Amos expected to meet his wife, who had arrived from California, to rejoin him after a three months' separation. I never have seen a man so nervous. He rode on the outside of the coach with the driver, that he might obtain the earliest view of the building that contained his adored one. It was with great difficulty that I kept pace with him as he "tumultuously rushed" up the step leading to the Rotunda. In an instant he was at the office and gasping "Mrs. Butterfield."

"In the parlor, Sir," replied Dan, and he was off.

I followed and saw him stop with surprise as he came to the door. In the centre of the parlor stood Mrs. Butterfield. That admirable woman had adopted the very latest and most voluminous style; and having on a rich silk of greenish hue, looked like a lovely bust on the summit of a new-mown haystack. Butterfield was appalled for a moment, but hearing her cry "Amos," he answered hysterically, "My Amander!" and rushed on. He ran three times round Mrs. Butterfield, but it was of no use, he couldn't get in. He tried to climb her, but the hoops gave way and frustrated the attempt. He extended his arms to her; she held out hers to him; tears were in their eyes. It was the most affecting thing I ever witnessed. Finally Mrs. Butterfield sat down, and Amos got behind the chair and kissed her, until their off-spring, by howling and biting the calf of his leg, created a diversion. They were very happy, so were the people in the parlor. Everybody appeared delighted; and a small boy, a year or two older than little Amos, jumped up and down like a whip-saw and halloa'd "Hoop-ee" with all his might.

"Butterfield," said I, an hour or two later, "I suspect that Mrs. Butterfield has adopted hoops."

"Oh! yes," answered he, "I saw that sticking out. Perhaps it will obviate the little tendency she had to blow up. I'm glad of it."

I had taken room No. 3683 in this establishment, and am a looker on in Vienna. To be sure my view is that usually termed, "the bird's eye." but I am getting a tolerably good idea of things. I should like very much to attend the ordination of Brother Buchanan in March next, and hear the Russian Minister preach, but I fear it will be impossible.

You will hear from me when you receive my next letter.

Respectfully yours,

JOHN PHOENIX

This rare, previously unpublished photograph shows an older, unbearded Derby in his First Lieutenant, 9-button, undress frock coat. This rather uncharacteristic photograph, circa 1855, may have been the inspiration of Derby's self-caricature which appeared as the frontispiece in Phoenixiana (1856).

SEWING MACHINE FELINE ATTACHMENT

Circular: to the Public

First printed in the Knickerbocker, July, 1857

PERMIT ME to call your undivided attention to an invention lately made and patented by myself, which is calculated to produce the most beneficial results, and prove of inestimable value to mankind. It is well known that the sewing-machines now so generally in use are the most important invention and greatest blessing of the age. Every lady considers this instrument indispensible to her happiness; it has completely usurped the place of the piano-forte and harp in all well-regulated families; and she who once purchased materials for clothing by the yard, now procures them by the piece or bolt to enjoy the rational pleasure of easily making them into garments.

In the humble cabin of the laborer, and in the halls of the rich and great, now resounds from morning until night, the whir of the sewing-machine. The result of this universal grinding, although eminently gratifying to the sellers of dry goods, and the philanthropic fathers and husbands who discharge their bills, has not been of a favorable nature to our ladies in a physical point of view. It is found that the constant use of the crank has brought on rheumatic and neuralgic affections in the shoulder, and a similar application of the treddle has a tendency to produce hip diseases, and white swelling of the knee-joint, accompanied by nervous complaints of a painful character. The undersigned is acquainted with a most estimable single lady of middle age, who, having procured one of the fast-running machines, was so enchanted with it, that she persisted in its use for thirty-six hours without cessation, and found, on endeavoring to leave off, that her right leg had acquired the motion of the treddle in such a painful manner that it was impossible to keep it still, and her locomotion therefore assumed a species of polka step exceedingly ludicrous to witness, and particularly mortifying to herself. I regret to add that she was compelled, by a vote of the society, to withdraw from the Methodist Church, on a charge of dancing down the broad aisle on a Communion Sunday.

A more melancholy instance was the case of Mrs. Thompson of Seekonk, a most amiable lady, beloved and respected by all around her, but who, by constant use of the crank, lost all control of the flexors and extensors of her right arm and inadvertently punched her husband in the eye, which, he being a man of suspicious and unforgiving disposition, led to great unhappiness in the family, and finally resulted in the melancholy case of Thompson *vs.* Thompson, so familiar to most of the civilized world.

A turn for mechanism, and an intense desire to contribute to the happiness of the female sex, have ever been distinguishing traits in my character. On learning of these facts, therefore, I devoted myself to a thorough investigation of the subject, and after a month of close application, have at last made an invention which will at once do away with every thing objectionable in the use of the sewing-machine.

This beautiful discovery is now named

"PHOENIX'S FELINE ATTACHMENT"

Like most great inventions, the Attachment is of great simplicity. An upright shaft is connected with the machine by a cog-wheel and pinion, and supported below by a suitable frame-work. Two projecting arms are attached to the shaft, to one of which a large cat is connected by a light harness, and from the other a living mouse is suspended by the tail, within a few inches of the nose of the *motor*. As the cat springs towards the mouse, the latter is removed, and keeping constantly at the original distance, the machine revolves with great rapidity. The prodigious velocity produced by the rapacity of the cat in its futile endeavors to overtake the mouse, can only be imagined by one who has seen the Attachment in full operation.

It is thus that man shows his supremacy over the brute creation, by making even their rapacious instincts subservient to his use.

Should it be required to arrest the motion of the machine, a handkerchief is thrown over the mouse, and the cat at once pauses, disgusted.

Remove the handkerchief and again she springs forward with renewed ardor. The writer has seen one (a tortoise-shell) of so ardent and unwearying disposition, that she made eighteen pairs of men's pantaloons, two dozen shirts, and seven stitched shirts before she lay down exhausted. It is to be hoped that the ladies throughout the land will avail themselves of this beautiful discovery, which will entirely supersede the use of the needle, and make the manufacture of clothing and household materials a matter of pleasure to themselves, and exciting and healthy exercise to their domestic animals. I present below an elevation of the "Feline Attachment" in operation, that all may understand its powers, and none fail to procure one, through ignorance of its merits. The Attachment will be furnished to families having sewing-machines, on the most reasonable terms, and at the shortest notice. Young and docile cats supplied with the Attachment, by application at 348 Broadway, New York. Office of the Patent Back-Action Hen Persuader.

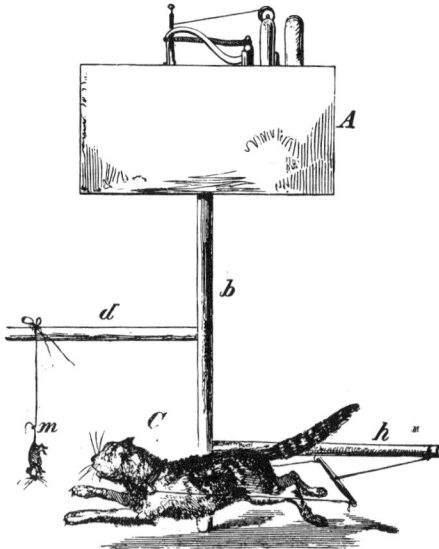

ELEVATION OF 'PHŒNIX'S FELINE ATTACHMENT.'

A. Sewing-Machine, Box-pattern,		$75 00
C. Cat, at various prices, say,		$2½ to 10 00
B. Vertical Shaft,		5 00
D. H. Projecting arms,		50
M. Mouse,		12½
Total cost of Machine and Attachment,		$90 62½

MASSACHUSETTS DENTAL ASSOCIATION

*First printed in the Boston Post,
August 10, 1857*

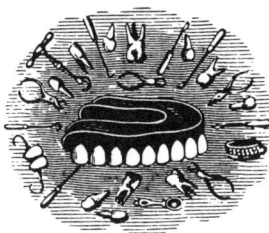

NAHANT HOUSE, August 6, 1857. While deeply interested in the discussion of the luxurious repast provided for the happy guests of this mansion yesterday afternoon, my attention was diverted by the sound of music of a wild and Saracenic description, resounding from the exterior of the building. The melody appeared to be that portion of the "Battle of Prague" which represents the "cries of the wounded," accompanied by an unlimited amount of exertion on the part of the operator on the bass drum.

Hastily rushing to the window, bearing elevated on my fork the large potato from which I had partially removed the cuticle, (Stevens gives us enormous potatoes, it takes twenty minutes to skin one properly) I beheld a procession, numbering some three or four hundred, all in their Sunday clothes, every man with a cigar in his mouth, slowly and solemnly moving past the hotel. They bore a banner at their head, on which was depicted an enormous cork-screw, or some instrument of that description, with the motto *"A long pull, a strong pull, and a pull all together."* Judge of my astonishment and delight in recognizing in the beam of this banner, my old friend, the philanthropic Tushmaker, of widespread dental renown. As the procession reached the front of the hotel, each man threw away his cigar, and having replaced it by a large quid of tobacco, defiled on the esplanade beneath the piazza in a tolerably straight line, and then gazing intently at the windows, opened his mouth, from one auricular orifice to the other, and showed his teeth.

Never have I seen so glittering a display. Filled with curiosity, I was about to ask an explanation when my friend Doolittle from Androscoggin, who had rushed to the window at the same time with myself, saved me the trouble by demanding with an incoherent and exceedingly nasal pronounciation, "Why, what on airth is this ere?"

"This," replied the courteous Hiram, whose suavity of manner is only equalled by the beauty of his person, "this, sir, is the American Dental Association, composed of members from all parts of both continents, and from the British West India Islands."

"Jerewsalem," said Doolittle, "three hundred tewth carpenters!"

It was indeed a thrilling spectacle. To think of the amount of agony that body of men had produced, and capable of yet producing, to think of the blood they had shed, and of their daring and impetuous charges, after the gory action was over! The immortal charge of the six hundred at Balaclava was not a circumstance to the charges made daily by this three hundred. As Hiram had truly said, these were dentists from all parts of the civilized world and elsewhere. There was the elegant city practitioner, with shiny hat and straw-colored gloves, side by side with the gentleman from the country, who hauls a man all over the floor for two hours for a quarter of a dollar, and gives him the worth of his money. I observed that forty-seven of them wore white hats, and two hundred and sixty-eight used tobacco in some form. There can be no question that this substance is a preservative to the teeth. I observed, in the rear rank, the ingenious gentleman who invented the sudden though painful method of extracting a tooth by climbing a tree and connecting by a catgut string the offending member with a stout limb, and then jumping down; a highly successful mode of operation, but not calculated to become popular in the community. He wore buckskin moccasins and did not appear to be enjoying a successful practice.

But while I gazed with deep interest upon the assembly, the band struck up *"Tom Tug"* and away they went. Three times they encircled the hotel, then, "with their wings aslant, like the fierce cormorant," swooped down upon the bar, registered their names and took a grand united Federal drink (each man paying for himself). Here toasts and sentiments were the order of the day.

"The American Dental Association, like watermen, we pull one way and look another."

"A three dollar cavity, very filling at the price."

"The woodcock, emblem of dentisty — he picks up his living from the holes and passes in a precious long bill."

"The memory of Dr. Beale."

These, with other sentiments of a similarly meritorious character, were given and received with great applause.

Having all drank from the flowing bowl, the association again formed in a line in front of the piazza, which were now crowded with a curious and admiring throng, and sang with surprising harmony the following beautiful, plaintive and appropriate chant —

1.

"Oh, Jonathan Gibbs, he broke his tewth
A eatin' puddin', a eatin' puddin' —
Jonathan Gibbs he broke his tewth
A eatin' puddin', a eatin' puddin'.

2.

"Great lumps of suet, they stuck intew it,
Intew it, intew it, intew it, intew it,
Great lumps of suet, they stuck intew it,
As big as my two thumbs."

This chant finished, and the applause subsiding, an air of gravity came over the association, and the president, Dr. Tushmaker, stepping forward, announced that a few pleasing and wonderful performances would now be gone through with the object of exhibiting the dexterity acquired by the members of the society.

Then turning to the line he gave the command, "*Draw!*"

In an instant every one of the association was armed with a brilliant turnscrew.

"*Fix!*" shouted Dr. Tushmaker, and each member opened his mouth and attached the fearful instrument to a back tooth.

"*Haul!*" screamed the doctor.

"Hold, for God's sake," shouted I, but it was too late; three hundred double-fanged teeth, dripping with blood, were held exultant in the air. The association looked cool and collected; there might have been pain but, like the Spartan boy, they repressed it. The ladies with a wild cry of horror, fled from the piazza.

"*Replace!*" shouted Dr. Tushmaker, and in an instant every tooth returned to the mouth whence it came. I understood it at once, it was ball practice with blank cartridge — they were all false teeth.

Several other interesting exercises were gone through. A hackman passing by on his carriage was placed under the influence of chloroform, all his teeth extracted without pain, and an entire new and elegant set put in their place, all in forty-two seconds. His appearance was wonderfully improved; he had been known, for years, as "Snaggled Toothed Bill," but a new and more complimentary title will have to be devised for him. Wonderful are the improvements of science. At five o'clock the procession was reformed, and the band played "*Pull, Brothers, Pull.*" The association moved off, returning by the *Nelly Baker* to Boston.

I have never seen three hundred dentists together before, and I don't believe anybody else ever did, but I consider it a pleasing and an improving spectacle, and would suggest that the next time they make an excursion which shall combine business with pleasure, they all go down together and remove the snags from the mouth of the Mississippi. Yours respectably,

J.P —

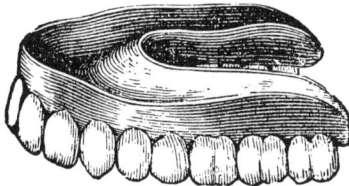

Illness and office work kept Derby in the vicinity of Boston, New York and St. Louis during most of 1857, but in November he was dispatched to construct lighthouses along the Alabama and Florida coasts. His friend Charles Poole faithfully accompanied him as clerk.

Derby and Poole arrived on November 2, and in his letter to his mother on November 6, 1857 Derby wrote that his eyesight had suddenly failed. "... Everything is very indistinct and I see all objects double... if I go blind he (Poole) will write my letters for me."

The tone of the following letter to Dr. Charles Hitchcock is frightened and the tasks Derby requests are those of a man tying up the loose ends of his estate.

Somehow Derby remained actively at work during most of 1858 and 1859, but as he labored under the tropical sun, he suffered a sunstroke, which further complicated his illness.

Doctors diagnosed his ailment as "amaurosis" but many of the symptoms — blurred vision, disorientation — indicate that Derby may have been suffering from a brain tumor. By the fall of 1859, Derby was unfit for further duty, and his old acquaintances barely recognized him. He seemed absent-minded, barely conscious of other people. On the Pacific Coast, rumors spread that the "mad wag" had gone insane.

LETTER TO CHARLES M. HITCHCOCK, M.D.

Letter Courtesy **The Bancroft Library**, **University of California**

Mobile, Ala. Nov 16, 1857

My Dear Friend,

I am suffering under an attack of what the Doctor calls an Amaurosis which prevents my reading and writing and I am obliged to employ Mr. Poole's eyes instead of my own.

I received your letter of the 5th October and at your request I enclose you the deed. I beg you will destroy this deed immediately and send me any note connected therewith to me by the return mail. Please do not fail to take this course as I do not wish to have the note kept longer in existence as if anything were to happen to either of us, it might prove a source of trouble.

I gave instructions to Capt. Stine to sell the house and pay Hyatt his eight hundred dollars which I hope will be done satisfactorily. If you write to Oliver F. Witherby at San Diego he will pay our taxes, my share of which I will send to you when I know what it is. I enclose a paper which Mary and I wish you to sign and return it to me by the first mail. Please get two witnesses to witness your signature.

Give my love to Mrs. Hitchcock and Miss Lily, who I hear has grown to be an elegant young lady.

Signature Cut Off

(Written for George Derby by Charles H. Poole)

LETTER TO MARY COONS DERBY

Mary Coons Derby accused her mother-in-law of spreading rumors that George Horatio was mentally deranged. In this letter from George Derby's uncle, Elias Hasket Derby Jr. (b. 1803), the noted statesman, author, and attorney, tries to quash falsehoods that George was insane and that his father, John Barton Derby, was a "drunken sot."

*(Letter Courtesy **The Bancroft Library, University of California**)*

Court St., Boston
Oct 21st, 1859

My dear Madam

Your favor of the 16th current is before me & I hasten to reply. I saw your husband early in the Autumn during his visit to Boston, his manner appeared a little different from his deportment previously. I should say that he moved with more rapidity and spoke apparently under a little excitement. He told me his eyes were better from the use of Belladonna & other potent medicines. I soon after saw Mr. Makepeace, the agent of Mrs. Derby & he told me that

Captain Derby had been a little irregular in his deportment & language that he ascribed it to the very potent medicines that he had taken as producing not derangement, but a temporary excitement & we both came to the same conclusion, although it is possible both have felt a little fear of more serious results. I am very glad to learn from your letter that I arrived at the right conclusion & infer from the way in which you speak of him that he is now with you. I doubt not that by your assiduous care he will regain his health and energies.

In your letter you say that his mother engaged his baggage for Boston Steamer while you were in New York, but do not say where he has been since that time, or whether he came to <u>Boston</u> & how he reached St. Louis. Please advise me.

I am happy to say that there is no hereditary insanity in the family. His father, grandfather and great Grandfather were men of sound mind & his Grandmother I have understood was a lovely woman & I have never heard of insanity in her family. As respects John B. Derby, the father of your husband, he was a man of brilliant talent & great energy, but he became a leading politician, obtained office, separated from his wife & formed a new connection. It is not for me to say that your husband's Mother was to blame, but I believe their tempers were incompatible & it does seem to me that she erred very much in judgment in not sending for you to meet him at Baltimore & in making a confidante of the Hotel Keeper. I will set the matter right here among his friends by stating that the Strychnine which he took for his eyes produced an excitement easily mistaken for a <u>slight derangement</u>.

As respects the statement that his father was deranged it is true that while in Office he became very intemperate & from his excesses became very ill & bedridden. I think he must have had a touch of paralysis. I joined with some friends and sent him to a "Water Cure" & his health was in a great degree restored, but he has been particularly while prostrated by his intemperance subject to certain slight hallucinations such as are common in light cases of Delirium Tremens & which I cannot consider insanity. He is now in a much improved condition.

By the death of his Step Mother he was entitled to receive at the discretion of his Father's Trustees about Forty-seven hundred dollars. This has been invested in a house where he now lives with his present wife & two very beautiful daughters & I presume they realize $400 to $500 each beside occupying a part of the house. He dresses well & presents a respectable appearance, appears calm and rational & writes at times beautiful poetry & is believed very temperate. I send you herewith some verses that he addressed a few days since to my Clerk Andrews, a very worthy man who has acted a kind part towards him & through whom, some of his kindred have aided him. I understand he has lately made a Will & consider him competent to do so. I am not surprised that your Husband is now depressed. It is the natural reaction. Keep him calm & tranquil. Let him live prudently & have the solace of your society & I doubt not you will restore him to health, both of body & mind.

Give my regards to him & please let me have more particulars.

Very sincerely yrs,

E. H. Derby

REQUEST FOR LEAVE OF ABSENCE

To Colonel John J. Abert,
Chief, Corps Topgl Engineers

Mobile 26 Nov 1859

Colonel

I have the honor to acknowledge the receipt of your letter of the 22nd in which you remind me that I neglected to furnish a reason for my application for leave of absence.* The reason that I have is a desire to improve in my profession, which I can do by examining the fortifications of Europe, and inspecting and studying the improvements in artillery, the newly invented guns, and the improvements in military engineering. You will observe that shortly after the expira-

---

* Editor's note — By late1859, Derby's illness had left him unable to read or write, suggesting irony in this letter outlining his reasons for requesting a leave of absence. Courtesy The Bancroft Library, University of California.

tion of the six months I shall be promoted by the fourteen year law to the rank of Captain in the Corps of Topographical Engineers. It is my earnest wish to fit myself thoroughly for this high position, and I think I can do this more thoroughly by a sojourn in Europe than by remaining in the U.S.

Still, if you have any active duty that you wish to put me on immediately, I shall be very happy to withdraw my application for leave of absence and go to work on such duty as may be assigned me.

I am, Sir
with high respect
Your obed. Servt

Geo H. Derby
Lieut Topgl Engrs.

Vum of Sand Island looking to the N.W

Vum of Sand Island looking to the S.E.

Derby Drawing Courtesy The Bancroft Library

Letter to Dr. Charles Hitchcock, of San Francisco

Squibob longed to return to California and seek medical help from Dr. Charles Hitchcock, who had saved his life as a cadet. But with three children (a second daughter, Mary, was born in Mobile, Alabama on April 23, 1858) Derby was unable to return to the West Coast.

Letter Courtesy **The Bancroft Library**, *University of California*

Wall House,
Williamsburg
August 15, 1860

My dear Friend,

I enclose a paper received from Judson Ames, showing our indebtedness for taxes on the lots in San Diego. Please pay this for me it is a trifle of $25.00 and I will remit you the money in gold. I have still great faith in San Diego making a fortune for us. * If the Southern route for the Pacific Railroad is taken & I have no doubt it will be, San Diego must be the terminus, and in that case our lots would be worth millions of dollars. Please attend to this promptly as we might otherwise lose our lots.*

Mrs. Hitchcock was here, but put out for Europe before we could see her. She stopped at the New York Hotel, I am sorry I never answered her beautiful letter to me, but I have been so sick that I could

*Editor's Note — Derby's daughter Mary inherited a few of these "priceless" lots that her father bought in the 1850's. When she died on August 7, 1893, her probate listed the assessed value of the property at $250.00.

not write. I am staying with Dr. Shittenpecker at his water cure in Brooklyn, N.Y. You may be pleased to hear how I get along. Mary is with me, also Daisy, both of whom are taking the water cure. Our fare is luxurious. We eat for breakfast two small rolls and a glass of milk. For Dinner we have two square inches of beef or mutton, half a potatoe with gravy and a teaspoonful of apple sauce, and a piece of bread. Supper — glass of milk and two small rolls. You may imagine I lose flesh on this weighing 142 lbs. I am pleased with this result as I shall shortly exhibit myself at Barnum's Museum as the Living Skeleton and make a handsome fortune as Barnum has promised me $30.00 a week when I get down to 30 lbs in weight. It won't be long. The Doctor eats for a breakfast a side of beef, 60 pounds of bread, a barrel of potatoes, 80 gallons of gravy & 360 eggs, also 460 slices of buttered toast. For dinner he has 800 sheep or 460 oxen, and for supper 120 lbs of beef or mutton with 4,000 lbs. of bread. We have no patients but Awful Arse Wood and Tailor or Tailerer who is getting thin every day. He will be my partner at the Museum.

Mrs. Derby will also go with me to the Museum as the woman with long hair. Oh, my lover is a Saileur Boy. I hope Mrs. Hitchcock will have a happy time in Europe, I am told Lily* is splendid, I have no doubt of it. I hope she will get well married. Mrs. Douglas is sick and at the point of death. I hope Douglas will marry Lily as there is no doubt he will marry Lily. Perhaps she will get the Prince of Wales and become Queen of England.

Dear Doctor I love you dearly and so does Mrs. Derby. We are anxious to see you. She is always talking about you. Write an answer to this letter that I may know that you have received it. I never expect to get back to California. Floyd promised to send me there but he had fizzled out. I wish I could go there again just to see you. I am told you are rich. I am a Captain by 14 years service. With the highest esteem & respect, your most affectionate friend,

Geo H. Derby
Captain, Topl Engineer.

*Editor's Note — Dr. Hitchcock's daughter, Lillie (1843-1924), became a belle of the San Francisco pioneer society and later married Charles Coit. When Lillie Hitchcock Coit died in 1924, she bequeathed a third of her estate to the City of San Francisco. The city used the money to erect a monument, known as "Coit Tower," to honor volunteer firemen.

LETTER
From
MARY
COONS
DERBY

On April 12, 1861 Fort Sumter was shelled and Captain Derby's West Point classmates and associates — McClellan, Jackson, Pickett, Lee, and Grant — were choosing sides in the American Civil War. But George H. Derby was spared the agony of the conflict. On May 15, 1861 "the Veritable Squibob" died and his remains were transported to that "worthless gambler town" St. Louis, Missouri.

*Letter to Dr. Charles Hitchcock, from the George Horatio Derby Papers, Courtesy **The Bancroft Library, University of California***

ST. LOUIS June 6, 1861

Dear, dear Doctor

Your letter of May 30th found me in the deepest affliction and desolation has emmersed herself in my heart — My noble and gifted husband is no more. Oh, could he but have been under your care I feel that he might have been saved — as I said in a former letter, his case was never understood here — they never reached the cause — Oh, how I wish it been you — to talk to all over. Can you believe that his bright intellect would have been so obscured? Do write me —

*tell me what you have heard as to the causes of his terrible disease,
but above all I wish to know your own theory in regard to his case.
Do you think the dissipated life he led for a few years could have
been the remote cause? * I can not give in to this, for it seems to me
the disease would have developed itself earlier — I am perfectly
familiar with those dark days, for he considered it his duty (so high a
sense of honor had he) to reveal every thing to me before marriage —
But the years of abstension that followed ought to have restored his
constitution — admitting it impaired by folly —*

*Do write to me and give me all the comfort you can. You arrived
in New York the very day my darling was interred — I brought his
remains to this city and they now repose in Bellefontaine Cemetary
— Oh, how dreary is this world (once so bright) to me now and
everyday I grow more and more weary of my pilgrimage. For over a
year I have had this terrible calamity hanging over me — and I have
lost him a thousand times. My nervous system has been strained to
the utmost and my faculties are fearfully impaired — what is to become of me I don't know — Do write me and tell me what conclusion you have drawn from what you have heard — I did wish so
much he could cross the plains, but he would not go without me —
nor would he go to Europe without me twice he had leave with permission to go beyond the confines of the United States — had I
known at the begining what I learned too late, I would have
sacrificed all my little ones rather than denied him the skill he would
have had access to over the other side — I am full of regrets &
reproaches — though my friends and the physicians assure me (in
their charity) I do myself injustice — that no one would have done
more and few could have acted as judiciously — but this does not
alter the condition of my mind — You can in some degree appreciate
my loss, for who knew him or loved him so well? — His friends.
Their name was legion, but to you he accorded the highest position in*

---

* Editor's Note — Some have suggested that George Derby suffered from a brain
tumor.

his heart — and I had the intensest longing to see you from the commencement of his disease.

I wish you would preserve for me any tribute that is paid in his memory in his beloved California. Oh, that we had never left there—

I trust you found affairs in better condition than you anticipated — and hope you will reach your house without any serious adventure.

Your elegant daughter I have reason to believe will realize your brightest hopes — Daisy* is more like her than any child I have ever seen —

Months ago I had a letter from Mr. Trevis a business letter, but I have had no heart to give it the attention it required — If I can I will enclose the deed to you.—

I cannot learn if Gen Hitchcock intends going to California — He is now at Green Bay — so sister tells me —

My dear & best of Mothers is blessed with health, but she feels keenly the deplorable condition of our country — She sends her love to you and I know of no one she would rather see —

Sister is to be married sometime this month — to Mr. Shaler, son of Judge Shaler of Pittsburg — I believe I have replied to all your inquiries —

I received two beautiful letters from your sister-in-law Mrs. Hunter of Georgia, but I cannot acknowledge them now.

My poor little boy Georgie is very much enfeebled by chills, but the others are well — Do write me a long letter when you can take the time —

With great respect

M.A.D.

* Editor's Note — George Derby's daughter Daisy Peyton, born in San Francisco December 3, 1854, married Lt. William M. Black, a young West Point officer. According to family history, Daisy committed suicide in Ashville, North Carolina on March 31, 1889, when her son Roger was four years old. Major General Black remarried and eventually became Chief Engineer of the U.S. Army Corps of Engineers.

LETTER TO DR. HITCHCOCK

Letter Courtesy **The Bancroft Library, University of California**

N. York
March 31, 1863

Dear Doctor,

I am about to inflict upon you another of my dull prosy letters, which I hope, however, you will have the patience to read when I tell you I shall expect no answer.

Having just heard that an impression prevails on the Pacific that George died of <u>hereditary insanity,</u> I hope after reading the enclosed letter you will take the trouble to do all in your power to correct the error — Mrs. Derby poisoned George's mind from the moment he could understand against his father and he died under the impression that his father was in an asylum — even reading the Hasket Derby letter which he was induced to write from inquiries made myself in reference to a declaration made by Mrs. Derby on shipboard at the Dinner Table — she asserted that her son was crazy (and his father

248

was before him) — and she was then on her way to a lunatic asylum with him — On receiving the letter written by the <u>Hotel Clerk</u> I started immediately from Boston and reached that city before Mrs. Derby who had kidnapped my husband at Baltimore — On meeting George I saw evidence of derangement and protested against such violent measures as his mother had resorted to and told her then that such a slip as she was taking would make a maniac of him.

She left no stone unturned to separate us when his very existence depended upon my presence for the Doctor assured her the only hope he had for her son was through the influence his wife had over him — Everything she did only made him more idolatrous towards his wife and weakened his affection for his mother —Ah, what I have suffered through that woman —

George sent her home from the Pacific because her jealous disposition allowed neither of us to have any peace — He sent her home from the Hyropathic Establishment for the same reason —and the Physician threatened to inform her that she must leave on the charge of mischief making, but at my intercession he gave up on this measure —

I have said much more upon this subject (Mrs. Derby) than I intended, but as often as I hear the circumstances of that summer and the high handed game played by Mrs. D —I am almost frantic — Why could she not have telegraphed me — could have been with him in <u>eight</u> hours. It would have been the first thing anyone else would have thought of — but no, she preferred to sacrifice her son to her animosity for me. In Baltimore George had an attack of <u>cerebral congestion.</u> Dr. Bunkler so pronounced it and said he was threatened with softening of the brain which he died with — and not insanity —

Please take good care of the letters enclosed and return them to care of Mr. G. Coleman —

I am going to Boston expressly to see George's Father — whom everyone pronounced as gifted as his son and far more elegant — which is saying a great deal —

Don't the poetry remind you of George? Remember the author was 72 years old. Is there anything about it to suggest <u>insanity?</u>

For the sake of my little children, I hope you will undo the mischief Mrs. D — Sr. has done —

Mr. Hasket D — is one of the most eminent lawyers in Boston and could have no object in writing me anything but the truth.

My little Daisy continues an invalid, and when I gaze upon the wreck of my once beautiful child it almost completes the destruction of my own mind — The intense anxiety with which I watched the decline of my idolized husband completely prostrated my nervous system that for four years I have not seen a well day — Ma thinks I am stubborn in refusing to submit myself to medical treatment, but when I think of the mistakes and blunders made in treating George I have no faith in Doctors. Moreover they cannot minister to a mind disabled —and my complaint comes under that head —

Georgy* reminds me more of his Papa than any of the children — and I must give you the benefit of a witty speech he made a few days since — The ends of Daisy's fingers have enlarged to such an extent that I remarked that she had a club from every finger.

George immediately replied "Well, Mama, if Clubs was Trumps what a hand Daisy would have."

For a six year old that is not so bad, think you?

He had Georgie's mouth and his magical smile —If he lives. I think he will make a splendid Topog — his idea of locality is wonderful — I send him in all directions, miles distant — I also think he will be a great mathematician — you cannot puzzle him in the multiplication table and he has a passion for figures —

---

* Editor's Note — Derby named his son after his West Point classmate George McClellan, the famous General from Pennsylvania. George McClellan Derby (born 1856, at sea) graduated first in his class from the United States Military Academy in 1878 and served as Chief Engineer with the Fifth Army Corps during the Spanish American War (1898). He was promoted to the rank of Colonel and was in charge of the Mississippi River Improvement during World War I (1917-1919). Unlike his father, George McClellan Derby lived a full life and died in 1948.

Mary is in St. Louis with Ma and Sister — they claim her entire-
ly — has George's teeth — and head, eyes and nose — yet she is
much too much like her Papa as his son —

Daisy says she don't think her Godfather care anything about her,
for he never writes or takes any notice of her — Did you know when
she was christened George had your name registered as her Godfather?

She told me the other day that she wished I would get something
historical for her to read — as she liked something she could believe.
Pilgrims Progress was only a dream after all. Get Josephine — she
should like that — or something about the Israelites.

I laughed — she is as old as the hills. Her conversational powers
are wonderful —

No Signature Attached

DERBY DIARY

1823: April 3: George Horatio Derby born, Dedham, Massachussetts
1842: July 1: Enrolled at West Point
1846: September- November: Harbor Survey, New Bedford, Mass.
    November: Drafting work in Baltimore, Maryland
    December 11: Ordered to Mexico with General Scott
1847: April 17: Wounded at Cerro Gordo
1847: July: Recovering from hip wound
1848: Spring: Upper Mississippi-Minnesota expedition
    November: Returns to Washington D.C. to prepare reports
    December 15: Derby ordered to California
1849: June 10: Arrives at Monterey, California
1849: July 5: Reconnaissance of Sacramento Valley with General Riley
    September 22: Bear Valley Expedition
1850: Jan — May Tulare Swamp Expedition, San Luis Obispo
    November: Colorado River Expedition on schooner *Invincible*
1851: March: Derby returns from exploration of Colorado River
    April 9, 1851: Derby organizes Sonoma Masonic Lodge
    August: Horse Thief incident, Sonoma, California
    November: Derby attempts suicide
1852: January - April: Duty in Sonoma and Benicia, California
    May 1: Derby returns to Boston, "The New Uniform" appears in *Carpet-Bag* magazine.
    October 24: Derby assigned to California in charge of "Turning the San Diego River into False Bay"
1853: January 8: Arrival in San Diego with Charles Poole, Assistant
    January - April: San Diego River Survey
    April 28: Derby Returns to San Francisco
    June 15: Squibob commits "Literary Suicide"

1853: July 12: Derby adopts *nom de plume* "John Phoenix"
August 10: Derby returns to San Diego aboard the *Northerner*
August 24: Judson Ames appoints Derby interim editor of San Diego *Herald*, and Derby urges readers to vote for the "John Phoenix Ticket"
October 1: "Illustrated Newspapers," John Phoenix, editor
1854: January 14: Derby marries Mary Angeline Coons
January 15: John Bigler inaugurated Governor of California
September 24: Derby requests transfer from San Diego
November: Derby reports to San Francisco
December 3: Daisy P. Derby born in San Francisco
1855: January - April: Benicia, California
July 17: Derby travels to Ft. Vancouver, Washington
October 2: Derby promoted to 1st Lieutenant, USTC
December: *Phoenixiana*, D. Appleton & Co., New York
1856: January - May: Derby in charge of roads, Oregon, California
June: Assigned to survey lakes with Kearny
October 21: Derbys leave California
November 1: George McCellan Derby born at sea
1857: January: Derby assigned Florida lighthouse duty, has sunstroke
May: Derby takes leave of absence
June- October: Lighthouse duty in Boston
July: Derby promoted to Captain, by fourteen year rule
November-December: Lighthouse duty in Mobile, Alabama
1860: November: Derby requests permission to leave the United States
1861: April 15: Guns of Fort Sumter
May 15: Derby dies of "softening of the brain"
1865: Derby's widow and Charles Poole publish *The Squibob Papers*
1897: Caxton Club edition of *Phoenixiana*
1899: January 31: Derby's remains reinterred, U.S. Military Academy at West Point. The inscription includes the line: "With thee vanished the light of my life my husband."

Photograph by Albert F. Reynolds

Richard Derby Reynolds is a descendant of the Derby family of Salem, Massachusetts, and he is a distant relative of Lt. George Horatio Derby, "the Veritable Squibob."

After graduating from Kenyon College, Gambier, Ohio, in 1970, Reynolds settled in San Diego where he began his writing career as a "muckraker" on the *San Diego Door*, an underground newspaper. Three years later Reynolds moved to San Francisco and wrote for the *Berkeley Barb,* reporting on topics such as the Patty Hearst kidnapping. He later produced a film documentary on the subject. In 1978 Reynolds received a special project grant from the California Arts Council and produced *Mudflat*, an award-winning half-hour documentary about mysterious art sculpture along the San Francisco Bay.

Reynolds returned to writing in 1983 with an article for *California Magazine* entitled "The Pendragon Chronicles," and in 1987 Reynolds published his first nonfiction book *Cry For War,* which detailed the murder rampage of Suzan and Michael Carson, the so-called "Witch killers of San Francisco."